CHAUCER'S DREAM-POEMS

By the same Author

*

THE MASTER-MISTRESS:
A STUDY OF SHAKESPEARE'S SONNETS

THE PLAYER KING:
A THEME OF SHAKESPEARE'S HISTORIES

CHAUCER'S DREAM-POEMS

By

JAMES WINNY

1973

CHATTO & WINDUS

LONDON

Published by
Chatto & Windus Ltd
42 William IV Street
London WC2N 4DF

*

Clarke, Irwin & Co. Ltd.
Toronto

ISBN 0 7011 2016 9 PAPERBACK
ISBN 0 7011 2000 2 HARDBACK

© James Winny, 1973

Printed in Great Britain by
Cox & Wyman Ltd.
London, Fakenham and Reading

For Arthur and Jean

CONTENTS

ACKNOWLEDGEMENTS

Like every recent student of Chaucer, I have been indebted from the outset to Robinson, whose text and notes have been at my elbow throughout the writing of this book. Among modern critics I have profited most from the work of Professor J. A. W. Bennett, Professor Wolfgang Clemen, Professor John Lawlor, and Dr. D. S. Brewer, whether I agreed with their readings of the poems or not. I have been helped in a different way by a grant of money from Leicester University, which covered some of the expenses incurred in the earlier stages of my work, and by my wife, whose encouragement has helped me to finish the book. To all these my grateful thanks are due.

J.W.

ABBREVIATIONS

The following abbreviations are used to identify quotations:

BD   *The Boke of the Duchesse*
CT   *The Canterbury Tales*
HF   *The House of Fame*
LGW   *The Legend of Good Women*
PF   *The Parlement of Foules*
RR   *The Romaunt of the Rose*
TC   *Troilus and Criseyde*

DL   *Le Dit dou Lyon*
FA   *Le Dit de la Fonteinne Amoureuse*
RB   *Le Jugement dou Roy de Behaingne*
RN   *Le Jugement dou Roy de Navarre*

Quotations from Machaut are taken from *Les Oeuvres de Guillaume de Machaut*, ed. Hoepffner, Paris 1908.

I

INTRODUCTION

CHAUCER's dream-poems present a special problem to under-standing and interpretation. In the commonsense world of the Canterbury pilgrims Chaucer's intentions seem initially as forthright as Harry Bailly's orders to his story-tellers; and when later this proves too trustful a view of the poet's purposes, at least the individual tales yield an immediately intelligible meaning as stories. The dream-poems do not. In Chaucer's fictional world as in real life, the dreamer's experience does not conform to the familiar standards of waking truth, but follows an erratic path which although perhaps obeying some curious inner logic seems entirely arbitrary and random. This random quality is not necessarily accidental. The dream-poem clearly appealed to its medieval writers partly because it allowed them to indulge a taste for the bizarre by devising the kind of un-fathomable happening which every sleeper knows. Chaucer evidently responded to this attraction of the dream-poem. His readers are not encouraged to overlook the oddity of his dreamers' adventures, and are even invited to marvel at their strangeness when in fact they involve nothing extraordinary. The dream described in *The Boke of the Duchesse* does not stretch credulity at all; yet the dreamer begins by declaring it so wonderful that no man – apart perhaps from the great authority Macrobius –

> had the wyt
> To konne wel my sweven rede.   [*BD* 278–9

His counterpart in *The Hous of Fame* has better reason for astonishment in the succession of marvellous sights and en-counters which his dream brings about. The great palace of Fame,

built throughout of beryl-stone, taxes his powers of description
by being

> so wonderlych ywrought
> That hit astonyeth yit my thought,
> And maketh al my wyt to swynke. [HF 1173-5

Although very different in materials and structure, the rotating
House of Rumour impresses the dreamer in much the same
way; and drawing on a shaky recollection of mythology he
asserts that not even 'that Domus Dedaly' called Laboryntus
was

> made so wonderlych, ywis,
> No half so queyntelych ywrought. [HF 1922-3

By stressing the 'wonderlych' or marvellous features of the
dream the poet admits his interest in making his audience share
this sense of awed astonishment: ultimately a tribute to his own
inventive power, even when the dreamer confesses himself
incapable of suggesting the unearthly richness or craftsmanship
of what he sees. 'Al the men that ben on lyve,' the dreamer
affirms during his account of Fame's house,

> Ne han the kunnynge to descrive
> The beaute of that ylke place. [HF 1168-9

A tradition which set such a value on wonder and strangeness
was likely to encourage poets to exploit these sensations without
regard to imaginative purpose, as though to be successful a
dream-poem should startle and mystify, not deepen its reader's
awareness. Because Chaucer's dream-poems evince this typical
concern to puzzle their audience, without offering any elucida-
tion of the odd experience which the dreamer undergoes, we
may suspect that he too may be merely exploiting a current
taste for incomprehensible oddity.

If this were so, Chaucer's remark about there being no one
with understanding enough 'to konne wel my sweven rede'
would be true in another sense, and attempts to resolve the
inner meaning of the dream-poems would be mistaken from the
outset. In fact Chaucer is less likely to have used the dream-

poem simply to arouse astonishment than other medieval poets, who did not share his intellectual interest in the theory of dreams and their interpretation. Although he habitually makes a joke of his learning, and implies that his preoccupation with books denies him knowledge of actual life, up to the date of *The Nun's Priest's Tale* dreamlore is a subject which he treats respectfully; and each of his dream-poems includes some discussion of the topic, considered against the dreamer's experience. In this respect Chaucer seems to have treated the tradition of the dream-poem in his own fashion. One might generalise and suggest that serious significance was to be expected of the medieval poet's vision only if, like *Pearl* and *Piers Plowman*, it had a spiritual or religious purpose. The love-vision, although in some respects parallel or analogous to the revelation provided by a divinely inspired dream, could have no such comparable meaning – except for the worshippers of Venus. It presented the form of an ideal, of love in its aristocratic perfection, and in surroundings or circumstances which heightened the reader's sense of reverential awe; assuming, that is, that he was himself a devotee of courtly love. Since the reader was already familiar with the ideal, the dream could be no more than an illustration, whose purpose was not to disclose hidden truth but to excite tender feelings by its beauty, pathos or delicacy.

The general form of the experience which the dreamer undergoes in a love-vision was effectively laid down in the second quarter of the thirteenth century by the French *Roman de la Rose*, which became the most influential of poems in this tradition. Chaucer's translation of the opening seventeen hundred lines of the *Roman* includes a description of the Garden of Love, one of the most persistent of backgrounds in medieval poetry, and shows the essentially static quality of the dreamer's adventure. It begins when the poet falls asleep at the end of a splendid day in early summer, and dreams of going into the country to enjoy the birdsong. In a grassy meadow near a river he comes across a square garden enclosed by high walls decorated with 'many riche portraitures' representing human attributes excluded from the Garden – Hate, Felony, Covetise,

Avarice, Envy and other qualities incompatible with its owner,
Mirth. The dreamer studies these pictures with deep interest,
and a descriptive passage well over three hundred lines long
holds up any further progress of the story. The example of this
absorbed study of an elaborate work of decoration or architecture was to be copied in many later dream-poems, with the
same immobilising of their narrative movement. Eventually the
dreamer searches for an entrance to the garden, and after
knocking for a long time upon a wicket gate he is answered by
a beautiful young woman, who introduces herself as Idleness
and explains that the lord of the garden is Mirth. The dreamer
begs to be allowed to see Mirth and his jolly companions, and is
admitted to the garden. His first impression is not of human
figures, but of a great flock of singing birds: 'nyghtyngales,
Alpes, fynches, and wodewales,' turtle-doves, larks

> That wery, nygh forsongen were;
> And thrustles, terins, and mavys,
> That songen for to wynne hem prys;   [RR 664–6

all singing with great accomplishment. After this joyous prelude he comes upon Mirth and his folk, attended by musicians
and singers: Gladness, Love, Courtesy, Beauty, Riches, and
others representing the qualities which properly accompany
such a lord. He is greeted by Courtesy, who invites him to join
their dance, led by Mirth. The dreamer's account of these
figures occupies six hundred lines of Chaucer's translation, after
which he turns his attention to the garden itself.

The trees are even more numerous and diverse in kind than
the birds. Pomegranate, nutmeg, almond, fig, date, clove,
ginger, cardomom and many other spices grow there, with
every sort of delicious fruit – peaches, quinces, apples, medlars,
plums, pears, chestnuts and cherries. The timber trees include
great elms and oaks, maple, ash, plane, aspen, poplar, yew and
lime; set apart from each other to allow full growth, so that their
branches join to form a roof of dense foliage. This provides
shade for the harmless wild creatures playing on the green
turf:

> There myght men does and roes yse,
> And of squyrels ful grete plente
> From bowe to bowe alway lepynge.
> Conies there were also playinge.   [RR 1401-4

Everywhere the dreamer hears the sound of running water from
wells and streams, devised by Mirth as an added source of
pleasure, bringing moisture to the flower-studded grass growing
in the soft earth of the garden. 'There sprang the vyolet al
newe,' the dreamer comments,

> And fressh pervynke, riche of hewe,
> And floures yelowe, white and rede;
> Such plente grew ther never in mede.   [RR 1432-4

By this point the dreamer has brought together most of the
features which recur in the background of love-visions over the
next two centuries. To put a stop to his account of the garden he
professes himself unable to give any adequate impression of its
unearthly beauty. 'I wol nat longe holde you in fable,' Chaucer
makes him declare.

> Of al this garden dilectable.
> I mot my tonge stynten nede,
> For I ne may, withouten drede,
> Naught tellen you the beaute al,
> Ne hald the bounte therwithal.   [RR 1440-4

The beauty and excellence of the garden have in fact been
described in great detail, but in these fourteen hundred lines of
verse the story has moved hardly at all. The dreamer has
walked into the meadows, discovered the garden, and knocked
at the gate for admittance. On this slight framework of event
the poet has hung three extended passages of description, two
consisting of 'portraitures' of courtly and uncourtly qualities,
and the third listing all the natural features of the garden:
passages virtually as static as the pictures painted on the
walls.

Such a dream, whose almost motionless elegance and charm

were to become typical of the love-vision, holds no cryptic significance and requires almost no interpretation. It offers an enchanting fantasy of human life divorced from all the disagreeable aspects of actual existence – old age, poverty and sorrow are among the conditions excluded from the garden – and made more attractive by music, birdsong, courtly pastimes and delightful company, in a setting of unimaginable natural beauty and richness. The only kind of revelation which the dream provides is seen in its personifications of human attributes: poverty, naked as a worm; avarice, poorly dressed in a ragged old coat,

> As she were al with doggis torn;   [RR 221

Mirth, with a face 'as round as appil', and Fraunchise, 'symple as dowve on tree'. The ideal necessarily involves disparagement of the lower classes, in whom the ugly and ignoble qualities are represented; and limiting the figures inside the garden to a single privileged milieu restricts the interest of the poem in a way which Chaucer was to find unacceptable. But there was much else in this traditional form of dream which conflicted with Chaucer's imaginative outlook; and although characteristic elements of the courtly vision appear in each of his three dream-poems,[1] the special interest of Chaucer's work in this genre derives from features of the dreamer's experience that are incompatible with the aristocratic ideal established by de Lorris and his followers. From the first, Chaucer shows himself unwilling either to accept a social limitation on his subject-matter or to treat courtly attitudes at their own valuation. In the third of his dream-poems the unruly crowd of lower-class birds who shatter the serenity of a conventional ideal threaten to impose their own uncouth standards on the mixed world of the dream, and are only checked by the authority of the goddess Nature.

---

[1] This study does not deal with the unfinished *Legend of Good Women* which, although beginning as a dream, uses the convention only to introduce its nine verse biographies of exemplary heroines of myth and classical history.

By admitting representative ideas and figures of common life to his dreamer's experience, Chaucer sets up tensions between the courtly and the plebeian, and between fantasy and the actual, which give his poems an intellectual interest generally lacking in the love-vision. This tension is an important feature of *The Boke of the Duchesse*, the earliest and most traditional of Chaucer's works in this genre; for here the interest of the dream centres upon the story of a courtly love-affair related to the dreamer by a despondent lover, whose long narrative anchors the poem to one spot from the point when the dreamer encounters him. The two later dream-poems have a much greater liveliness, both of spirit and of action. The swift descent of the Eagle in *The Hous of Fame* is an event which the dreamer can only represent by the most violent of comparisons. 'Never was ther dynt of thonder,' he asserts,

> Ne that thyng that men calle fouder,
> That smot somtyme a tour to powder,
> And in his swifte comynge brende.   [HF 535–7

Later in the same poem he calls upon similar images of thunderous noise and rapidity to describe the whirling House of Rumour:

> And ever mo, as swyft as thought,
> This queynte hous aboute wente,
> That never mo hyt stille stente . . .
> And the noyse which that I herde,
> For al the world, ryght so hyt ferde
> As dooth the rowtynge of the ston
> That from th'engyn ys leten gon.   [HF 1924–34

A love-vision is not the likeliest source for a reference to a military catapult or to a thunderbolt; but by the date of this poem Chaucer's imagination had acquired a dynamic energy which could not be accommodated to courtly sensibility alone. The central character of a dream-poem is necessarily confined to the role of spectator. He is a visitor, admitted to an attractive but alien world as a reporter of its wonderful people and buildings;

B

a listener and onlooker who cannot become personally involved in its situations. From the reader's point of view he
may disappear altogether in the long descriptive passages
which require nothing of him except an account of the fabulous
events and objects he encounters. Himself a generally static
figure, his main task is to evoke an impression of almost motionless beauty in a changeless world. This would not be Chaucer's
way. When the dreamer in *The Boke of the Duchesse* throws himself from his bed into the saddle, to gallop impetuously after the
'gret route' of hunters and foresters whose noise has roused him,
Chaucer is showing a typical disinclination to accept the inertia
which threatens most dream-poems – a condition which in fact
settles upon this work when the hunt ends without a kill. The
two later poems include characteristically static situations when
the dreamer describes in detail a great painting or a splendid
garden; but in both works this rapt contemplation is prelude to
a dynamic happening which allows Chaucer to exploit an
imaginative interest in physical activity, conflict and comic
disorder: a concern which would in time assume a dominant
position in his work.

The developing energy of Chaucer's writing gave him reason
to approach the traditions of the love-vision with something less
than complete respect. His scholarly curiosity about the nature
and causes of dreams evidently impelled him to reshape the
tradition to his own purposes. In none of his three dream-
poems does he seem attracted by the prospect of merely evoking
wonder by incidents or figures which have no other *raison
d'etre*. The mind of his dreamer is at work puzzling over his
adventure and trying to fathom its significance. When the
narrator in *The Hous of Fame* feels mystified by the astounding
'noblesse of ymages' in the richly decorated Temple of Venus,
he tries to discover the identity of their creator and his own
whereabouts:

> 'But now wol I goo out and see,
> Ryght at the wiket, yf y kan,
> See owhere any stiryng man
> That may me telle where I am.'   [HF 476–9

Similarly when Africanus appears to him in his sleep at the end
of a day spent poring over the *Somnium Scipionis*, the dreamer
recognises the need for an explanation of the event and
diffidently offers a suggestion:

> Can I not seyn if that the cause were
> For I hadde red of Affrican byforn,
> That made me to mete that he stod there.
>
> [PF 106–8

Chaucer knows well enough that this is the obvious cause of
such an associative dream, but does not allow his typically
ungifted dreamer to be very assertive about the idea. However,
the comment indicates a wish not to be entirely ignorant about
the pyschological impulse of his dream, which is not to be
regarded simply as an odd and unaccountable happening but
as an experience to which the sleeper's mind contributes
images and motifs. Because Chaucer's dreamer is usually a little
slow-witted, his attempts to understand the working of his
mind during sleep are often half-comic; but the comedy of the
situation masks an interest on Chaucer's part which is evidently
serious. In this view, dreams are much more than fantastic
mental collages. They embody in bizarre and cryptic form
aspects of truth hidden from waking consciousness, in which the
dreamer may recognise his problems or his personal situation
represented. For Chaucer the dream-poem seems to have provided a means of understanding the creative process on which
his work depended.

As the argument between Chauntecler and Pertelote shows,
medieval opinion about the worth and importance of dreams
was sharply divided; but since some of the most remarkable
stories involving prophetic dreams had the authority of holy
writ, the sceptical argument was obviously at a disadvantage.
Whatever Chaucer's private opinion about the worth of
dreams, he had the good fortune of being acquainted with some
of the most respected works on dreamlore; in particular with
the foremost medieval study of the subject, the amplified
Somnium Scipionis. This work of mixed authorship consisted in

greater part of a commentary by the fourth century Macrobius
on a dream described in Book VI of Cicero's *De re publica*;
and throughout the Middle Ages its analysis of the different
kinds of dream and their significances was universally
respected. Chaucer's first reference to Macrobius, identifying
him as

> He that wrot al th'avysyoun
> That he mette, kyng Scipioun,
> The noble man, the Affrikan,   [BD 285-7

is muddled in substance as in syntax: Scipio was not a king,
Macrobius did not relate his dream, and the 'Affrikan' concerned was the dreamer's famous grandfather Scipio Africanus,
who acts as guide in the vision. Evidently Chaucer's knowledge
of the *Somnium* at this date had not progressed beyond hearsay.[1]
By the time of writing *The Parlement of Foules* Chaucer was
better informed about the work, and able to summarise Scipio's
dream fairly exactly. The old book which his dreamer spends
the day reading is correctly ascribed to 'Tullyus' and not to
Macrobius, whose respect for the work is mentioned.[2] There are
no direct allusions to the *Somnium* in *The Hous of Fame*, which
begins with a long profession of ignorance about the different
types of dream and their causes; but the passage could only
have been written by someone familiar with the categories –
broadly prophetic and fantasmal – devised by Macrobius.
'Why that is an avisioun,' the dreamer remarks,

> And this a revelacioun,
> Why this a drem, why that a sweven,
> And noght to every man lyche even;
> Why this a fantome, why these oracles,
> I not.   [HF 7-11

---

[1] A reference to the *Somnium* in the opening lines of RR has a general
likeness to the passage in BD: 'An authour that hight Macrobes,/That
halt nat dremes false ne lees,/But undoth us the avysioun/That whilom
mette kyng Cipioun' – RR 7-10. This does not mention Africanus.

[2] 'Of which Macrobye roughte nat a lyte' – PF 112: probably referring
to Macrobius' opinion that 'there is nothing more perfect than this work,
in which the whole of universal knowledge is contained'.

His uncertainty is not altogether shared by Chaucer, who is
amusing himself by feigning ignorance in a way which reveals
his actual knowledge of the subject. In denying that he ever
troubles his mind 'to besily to swinke'

> To knowe of hir signifiaunce
> The gendres, neyther the distaunce
> Of tymes of hem, ne the causes,   [HF 17–19

the speaker at least discloses an awareness that dreams are
classified in 'gendres', each distinct from the others, and that the
interpretation of dreams takes the hour of their occurrence into
account. As he continues, ostensibly offering detailed proof of
how little he knows, the speaker runs through an exhaustive list
of the circumstances held to induce dreams; asking whether
they have physical causes such as 'folkys complexions' or

> to gret feblenesse of her brayn,
> By abstinence, or by seknesse,
> Prison, stewe, or gret distresse,
> Or ellys by dysordynaunce
> Of naturel acustumaunce.   [HF 24–8

On the other hand, he continues, perhaps dreams are brought
about by spiritual forces; in particular by the soul, which in its
perfection knows how future events will fall out,

> And that hyt warneth alle and some
> Of everych of her aventures
> Be avisions, or be figures   [HF 46–8

too darkly cryptic to be understood without special guidance.
The whole passage of some fifty lines, which concludes by
commending the subject to those 'grete clerkys' who may com-
prehend it, runs expertly over the whole field of discussion and
summarises its issues with the familiarity of a student closely
acquainted with current beliefs and theories. In pushing the
topic aside as too deep for him, the dreamer adopts an attitude
similar to that of Pandarus, who in Book V of *Troilus and Criseyde* reveals much the same familiarity with medieval opinion

about the causes and meanings of dreams; arguing that the
uncertainty of the matter should encourage Troilus to ignore
them. 'Ther woot no man aright what dremes mene,' he affirms,

> For prestes of the temple tellen this,
> That dremes ben the revelaciouns
> Of goddes; and as wel they telle, ywis,
> That they ben infernals illusiouns   [TC V. 365-8

– that is, fantasies produced by evil spirits. On the other hand,
Pandarus continues, physicians assert that dreams have entirely
physiological causes, 'complexiouns . . . or fast, or glotonye';
and these are not the only explanations. Others believe

> that thorugh impressiouns,
> As if a wighte hath faste a thyng in mynde,
> That thereof comen swich avysiouns;
> And other seyn, as they in bokes fynde,
> That after tymes of the yer, by kynde,
> Men dreme, and that th'effect goth by the moone.
> [Ibid., 372-7

Although a sceptic, Pandarus' knowledge of the theory of dreams
is as extensive as that of Chaucer's narrator in the earlier *Hous of
Fame*, who professes to know nothing about the subject. Characteristically, Chaucer makes this comic figure apologise for his
ignorance while his remarks show his expertise in a field of
study which the poet had made his own.

Although we should not suppose that Chaucer's dream-poems
could be explained in terms of Macrobius' beliefs, references to
his learned commentary and the categories he proposes may
leave us feeling that without a knowledge of the *Somnium* we may
miss some part of Chaucer's intentions. For a modern reader the
most immediate interest of Macrobius' commentary lies in its
third chapter, where the author classifies and describes five
different types of dream. Of these, three are to be taken seriously
and two have no significance in Macrobius' view. The three
important kinds – the *oraculum*, the *somnium*, and the *visio* – are
alike prophetic, differing in their manner of foreshadowing

future events. The *visio* is the simplest of them. The dreamer
sees the form of an experience which later comes about just as
the prophesy foretold. This straightforward prediction of the
future is well illustrated by Chauntecler's unnerving dream of a
creature who

> wolde han maad areest
> Upon my body, and wolde han had me deed.
>
> [CT VII. 2900–1

Chauntecler's graphic description of a reddish, furry animal
with slender muzzle and sharp eyes enables us to recognise a
prophetic anticipation of the fox whom he is to encounter later
that day, not surprisingly for the first time. The *somnium* does
not provide such a direct view of what is to come, but veils its
predictions by giving them cryptic or allegorical form which
only a skilled interpreter can explain. The last of the Monk's
tragic anecdotes provides a good example of such a dream, fore-
telling the end of Croesus through enigmatic figures which seem
to promise him good fortune:

> Upon a tree he was, as that hym thoughte,
> Ther Juppiter hym wessh, bothe bak and syde,
> And Phebus eek a fair towaille hym broughte
> To dryen hym with.
>
> [Ibid., 2743–6

But Croesus' daughter reveals the true significance of the dream
by warning him that it foretells his death by hanging. The tree
represents the gallows, and the two gods the extremes of weather
to which his body will be exposed: 'Reyn shal thee wasshe, and
sonne shal thee drye.' Another example of the *somnium*, also
involving a tree, is glanced at during Chauntecler's defence of
dreams, when he speaks of reading in the life of St Kenelm how
this infant son of a king dreamt of his own murder:

> A lite er he was mordred, on a day,
> His mordre in his avysioun he say.
>
> [Ibid., 3113–14

Chaucer does not offer any further details, but Caxton's *Golden Legend* tells how Kenelm saw himself climbing to the top of a great tree which was then felled by one of his close friends, and how Kenelm then flew to heaven in the shape of a little bird. As the child was too young to grasp the meaning of his dream, his nurse revealed its significance to him 'every deel'

> and bad hym for to kepe hym weel
> For traisoun;
>
> [Ibid., 3116–17

but despite this forewarning Kenelm could not avoid the fate which his *somnium* represented in typically allusive form.

Macrobius' third type of prophetic dream, the *oraculum*, differs from the *visio* and the *somnium* in two important respects. First, the dreamer does not himself see a pre-enactment of future events but is told what is to come about; and secondly, he is taken in charge by a spiritual instructor or guide for whom he feels great awe and reverence: a priest, a famous ancestor, or a god. In both respects the *oraculum* has close parallels in classical literature where an epic hero seeks advice about the future from the shade of a great seer or blood-relation. Although neither Odysseus nor Aeneas is asleep during the meeting with the shadowy guardian whom each consults, there are obvious similarities between these encounters in Hades and the equally momentous meetings of dreamer with ancestor which identify the *oraculum*. The likeness is probably more than coincidental; for as Anchises in the *Aeneid* prefaces his account of the future history of Rome by describing how the souls of the dead are morally regenerated, so does Africanus instruct his grandson Scipio in the same matter. Other correspondences between the two stories suggest that the *oraculum* derives much of its distinctive character from epic tradition. It may seem paradoxical that despite its title Scipio's dream is not a *somnium* at all; but Macrobius was concerned to put a Christian interpretation on the disclosure of divine purposes which forms part of Africanus' discourse, and probably for this reason he describes the dream as a *somnium*, arguing that 'the truths revealed to Scipio were couched in words that hid their profound meaning and could not be comprehended without skilful interpretation.'[1]

Macrobius recognises however that the dream is a typical *oraculum*, since it provided a detailed forecast of Scipio's future life as consul, general and statesman, and that the two figures through whom the dreamer learnt of these events – his father and his grandfather by adoption – were both revered for their piety, and associated with the priesthood. For good measure Macrobius adds that since the dream showed Scipio 'the regions of his abode after death, and his future condition', it may also be considered a *visio*. By combining all three types of prophetic dream, the *Somnium Scipionis* justified the special attention which Macrobius attracted to it by his commentary.

For Chaucer the *oraculum* seems to have held less interest than the two other kinds of precognitive dream, except as a form which could be exploited to comic advantage. Although *visio* and *somnium* find appropriately serious places in the poems, the most solemn and impressive of prophetic dreams appears not to have suited his imaginative purposes; and when he provides a summary of the *Somnium* in *The Parlement of Foules* he omits much that is characteristic of the special nature of the *oraculum*; in particular its direct revelation of future events, and its disclosure of the hidden workings of divine purpose. In the *Somnium*, Scipio is carried by his guides to a point above the planetary spheres, from which he looks down upon the insignificant body of the earth and outwards upon the immensity of the heavens; and he learns from Africanus what different fates await the souls of those who have dedicated themselves to their country's service, and of those who have surrendered themselves to appetite. As though acknowledging Macrobius' opinion that the purpose of the *Somnium* is, 'to teach us that the souls of those who serve the state well are returned to the heavens after death, and there enjoy everlasting blessedness.'[2]

[1] Macrobius, *Commentary on the Dream of Scipio*, tr. W. H. Stahl, New York, 1952; p. 90.
[2] Stahl, *op. cit.*, p. 92.

Chaucer is appreciably more explicit about Africanus'
description of the afterlife than about his precise forecast of
Scipio's future career, which Chaucer's summary whittles down
to a single line; 'And warnede hym beforn of al his grace.' The
importance given to spiritual revelation in the *oraculum* may
have made it difficult for a poet of Chaucer's persistently comic
outlook to put this type of dream to serious use. In the two
dream-poems whose guide transports and instructs the dreamer
in the general manner of the *oraculum* Chaucer obviously does
not intend to evoke a sense of solemnity, for the Eagle and the
Africanus of *The Parlement of Foules* are both jovial figures,
disrespectful towards the dreamer and – despite their function –
firmly associated with the world of everyday fact.

The two remaining types of dream recognised by Macrobius
are non-prophetic, and one of them is nonsensical. The *insomnium* is an associative dream, induced by the activities or preoccupations of the sleeper's waking experience, or by physical
needs which present themselves to his sleeping mind. Thirst and
hunger produce dreams of searching for food, or of drinking
copiously. A similar kind of compensating *insomnium* is provided
for the disappointed lover when he dreams of possessing his
mistress, or for a man in public life when he dreams of being
appointed to a high office. Other forms of *insomnium* protract
the anxieties of the day, continuing to prey upon the sleeper's
mind and not permitting him to lose sight of his waking distrac-
tions. Borrowing from Macrobius, Chaucer gives various
examples of such associative dreams, which merely reflect the
sleeper's immediate past:

> The wery huntere, slepynge in his bed,
> To wode ayeyn his mynde goth anon;
> The judge dremeth how his plees been sped,
> The cartere dremeth how his cartes gon.[1]

[PF 99–102

---

[1] In Macrobius the passage runs: 'The hunter lays his tired limbs upon
the bed, yet his mind returns to the wood and to his quarry. Sleep [brings
back] lawsuits to judges, and the chariot to the charioteer'. The translation is by D. S. Brewer in his *Parlement of Foulys*, London 1960; p. 103.

The same associative principle might explain why the narrator of this poem dreams that Africanus is standing by his bedside, when the day has been spent in studying Scipio's dream; but the speaker does not fully commit himself to this idea, which would allow his dream to be regarded as a meaningless *insomnium*. Africanus himself is not prepared to be treated as a mere chance of association, for he explains that the dreamer's respect for 'myn olde bok totorn' has earned him the reward of a vision fit for a poem. The dream which follows is not prophetic, but it brings the sleeper special insight or illumination broadly parallel to the disclosures of spiritual truth provided by the *oraculum*. In this different context the dreamer's guide has a function as instructor which combines comic levity with a serious purpose not to be expected of an *insomnium*.

Although the least significant for Macrobius, for the reader of medieval poetry the last type of dream is perhaps the most interesting and suggestive; though it revives the question whether any underlying meaning should be looked for in the random happenings of the dream-poem. The *visum* or *phantasma* – Chaucer's 'fantome' – seems to have a source in physical disorders such as indigestion, and to occur not during deep slumber but in the uncertain halfway stage between sleeping and awake. Where the *insomnium* at least reflects the preoccupations of the waking mind, the *phantasma* bears no intelligible relation to the dreamer's waking experience, but merely brings a crowd of fortuitous mixed and disordered images before him. 'In this drowsy condition,' Macrobius explains, 'the sleeper thinks he is still fully awake, and imagines he sees spectres rushing at him or wandering vaguely about, differing from natural creatures in size and shape; and hosts of divers things either delightful or disturbing.'[1]

By admitting that one type of dream was entirely meaningless, and induced by a commonplace upset, Macrobius gave the sceptic an excuse for regarding all dreams as fantasmal. The traveller in Chauntecler's tale of disaster at sea mocks his

[1] Stahl, *op. cit.*, p. 89.

friend's warning dream and insists upon continuing his voyage,
arguing that

> swevenes been but vanytees and japes;
> Men dreme alday of owles and of apes,
> And eek of many a maze therwithal;
> Men dreme of thyng that nevere was ne shal.
>
> [CT VII. 3091–4

His mockery would certainly be justified if he were speaking of
the *phantasma*, which consists only of delusive fancies and
grotesquely unnatural figures; for such dreams indicate nothing
beyond the deranged state of the victim's constitution. There is
some excuse for Pertelote's scornful reaction when her lover
relates his nightmarish vision of a creature with glowing eyes
and reddish fur who wants to kill him; for in her ignorance of
the fox's appearance she reasonably supposes that he has been
frightened by a typically fantasmal projection. Instead of
recognising a prophetic dream, she diagnoses a physical disorder caused by an over-abundance of choler, which produces
dreams

> Of arwes, and of fyr with rede lemes,
> Of rede beestes, that they wol hem byte,
>
> [Ibid., 2930–1

and prescribes a laxative to restore the healthy balance of the
bodily humours. Where a dream was correctly identified as a
phantasma, Macrobius might approve both the diagnosis and the
course of treatment, and would certainly agree that nothing
could be learnt from the weird and unearthly forms of such a
nightmare.

But a poet might feel more interest in the *phantasma*, recognising that its characteristic figures, 'differing from natural
creatures in size and shape', and its crowds of 'divers things
either delightful or disturbing', were more akin to the stuff of
his own dreams than those of the *visio* or the *somnium*. Although
in Macrobius' categories the importance of a dream was reckoned by its prophetic content, in poetry this quality was less
appealing than the element of the unusual and the marvellous

which the traditional love-vision supplied; and as Macrobius'
description of the *phantasma* shows, this type of dream, with its
crowd of fantastic beings 'that nevere was ne shal', came closest
to the strange experience which such poems habitually related.
It could not be a shortcoming of the poet's dream that it
involved freakishly unnatural creatures, but a commendable
feature to be stressed as though to heighten the reader's admira-
tion of the work. In the Hall of Fame Chaucer's dreamer sees
such a being, 'perpetually ystalled',

> A femynyne creature,
> That never formed by Nature
> Nas such another thing yseye.   [HF 1365-7

His claim is borne out by the bizarre picture presented by the
next twenty lines, which describe the goddess constantly varying
in stature between pigmy and colossus, covered with eyes, with
as many

> upstondyng eres
> And tonges, as on bestes heres   [HF 1389-90

and with partridge-wings growing from her feet. Like the spectral beings of the *phantasma*, the goddess is an arbitrary compilation of features such as the mind brings together when it is only
half-awake, and puzzling rather than illuminating. This dream
has a second characteristic of the *phantasma* in the crowds of
innumerable creatures and objects which swarm about the
dreamer. 'What shuld I make lenger tale,' he asks,

> Of alle the pepil y ther say,
> Fro hennes into domes day?   [HF 1282-3

Expanding his remark later, he comments that the Hall was as
full

> Of hem that writen olde gestes
> As ben on trees rokes nestes;   [HF 1515-16

a comparison which nicely establishes his affinity with the
everyday world. The building which contains this great

multitude of suitors to Fame has as many windows 'as flakes falle in grete snowes', and is decorated with figures of minstrels, trumpeters, and other musicians, 'moo than sterres ben in hevene'; while in the House of Rumour he becomes part of a human assembly so vast

> That certys, in the world nys left
> So many formed by nature,
> Ne ded so many a creature.   [HF 2038–40

The sheer oddity of much of the dreamer's adventure, and the unaccountable strangeness of much that he sees – the House of Rumour, although spinning ceaselessly, is sixty miles long – again suggests the *phantasma* by defying interpretation, but with a difference. The very qualities which relegated this type of dream to the least important of Macrobius' categories, apparent meaninglessness and incomprehensibility, assume a different value in a literary context, where to excite interest in his dream the poet could assert that not even the greatest authority on dreamlore could interpret it.

There was a further reason why the *phantasma* should make a special appeal to the poet. The cause of dreams, like the question of their importance, was continually being debated; and whether it was argued that they were induced by over-eating, waking impressions or evil spirits, the problem remained of just how their fictional happenings and figures were produced in the mind. Although almost nothing was currently known about the workings of the mind, it was not difficult to see that it responded to two different kind of stimulus, one in the external world and the other apparently within itself; and that when its sensitive apparatus of perception was upset by illness, lack of sleep or prolonged distress, it produced hallucinations instead of true reports. Such errors of the mind were much akin to dreams. Like them, they were induced by exhaustion, ill-health, or other circumstances which the narrator of *The Boke of the Duchesse* sees enfeebling the brain,

> By abstinence, or by seknesse,
> Prison, stewe, or gret distresse,   [HF 24–5

and again like dreams, in the sceptic's view, they corresponded
to nothing in reality. But the poet had experience of another
kind of hallucination, clearly related to dreams and the illusions
produced by sickness or strain, but distinct from them in the
pleasurable excitement and the impulse of creation which
accompanied it. His experience, later described as imaginative,
is more like the *phantasma* than the other kinds of dream, which
either provide prophetic visions of the future or extend the
sleeper's engagement with everyday affairs. Moreover, the
typical occurrence of the *phantasma* on the threshold of sleep,
when the mind is still half-conscious of the real world but
absorbed by the strange behaviour of spectral figures, seems to
offer a close parallel to the state of imaginative excitement in
which the poet apprehends, or is given, the matter of his poem.
The question arises whether Chaucer may not have used the
conventions of the love-vision to describe not a fictional dream
but an actual imaginative experience, whose general form and
character had much the same fantasmal nature.

The evident vagueness of medieval thinking about the creative imagination makes it more likely that the poets of the age
did not observe any clear distinction between different forms of
analogous mental experience. Although the term 'imagination'
was in use, it was very seldom used to denote the creative power
of the mind, and Chaucer himself seems not to have regarded
the word as having this meaning. He makes the speaker in *The
Boke of the Duchesse* refer to the 'sorwful ymagynacioun' which
preoccupies him, probably with the sense only that melancholy
thoughts possess him. A different meaning is involved in *The
Miller's Tale*, whose narrator remarks that men 'may dyen of
ymaginacioun' or of an absurd fancy; here the notion that a
second Flood is about to drown the world. In a third context.

> How hadde this cherl ymaginacioun
> To shewe swich a problem to the frere?
>   [CT III. 2218–19

the term implies a more purposeful activity of the mind, and
acquires associations with inventiveness and ingenuity. These

associations are carried a step further in *The Nun's Priest's Tale*, whose narrator describes how the fox,

> By heigh ymaginacioun forncast,
> The same nyght thurghout the hegges brast
> Into the yerd

[CT VII. 3217–19

foreknowing that he would find dinner there, though not that he would also lose it. This attribution of precognitive power to imagination is unusual, going beyond the definition given by Trevisa in 1398, which describes it as a faculty whereby 'the soule biholdeth the liknesse of bodily thing is that beth absente'.[1] Evidently he is speaking only of the reproductive imagination, which does not create new forms but calls up images of material objects seen previously. This is the power to which Boethius refers when he speaks, in Chaucer's translation of the *De consolatione*, of the characteristic activity of imagination: 'Also ymaginacioun, albeit so that it takith of wit the bygynnynges to seen and to formen the figures, algates though that wit ne were nat present, yit it envyrowneth and comprehendith alle thingis sensible.'[2]

These 'thingis sensible' correspond to the 'bodily thingis' of Trevisa's definition, and show again the limited medieval view of imagination as a power hardly distinguishable from memory, and capable only of summoning up images of material objects. The primary meaning now attached to the term – 'the creative faculty of the mind in its highest aspect; the power of framing new and striking intellectual conceptions; poetic genius' – appears not to have been current until the early sixteenth century.

It becomes a question whether in Chaucer's lifetime the language provided a means of referring unmistakably to the imagination in this now established sense; and beyond that, whether poets of the age were properly conscious of this faculty in themselves. Medieval psychology had not progressed beyond

[1] *De proprietatibus rerum*, III. iv. tr. 1398; Tollemache MS.
[2] *Boece*, V. prosa 4, 205–9.

assigning three 'sapiences' or mental powers to the brain;
memory, intellect, and engine. The last of them usually signifies
ingenuity or mother-wit, as it does in Pandarus' speech telling
Criseyde of his difficulty in keeping Troilus alive:

> For neither with engyn, ne with no loore,
> Unnethes myghte I fro the deth hym kepe.
>
> [TC ii. 565–6

Here 'engyn' implies a talent for devising schemes, as opposed
to 'loore' or traditional precepts. The term occurs again in
Chaucer's preface to his *Astrolabe*, where he confesses that the
book is a compilation drawn from the writings of old astro-
nomers, and not an original work 'of my labour or of myn
engyn'. Had the treatise been his own composition, it would
evidently have demonstrated the power of Chaucer's 'engyn' or
native talent. In this context the term acquires something of the
sense of a creative faculty, though one limited to the presentation of scientific facts, and lacking the impetus of 'feeling
profound and vehement' which Coleridge was to declare characteristic of imaginative power. There is only one reference to
'engyn' in Chaucer's work which seems to intend an allusion to
this creative force; a limitation explained by the prevailing
obscurity about the subject. It appears in the Proem to Book II
of *The Hous of Fame*, where the poet calls upon his powers to
prove themselves by describing the wonders which he encountered in his dream:

> O Thought, that wrot al that I mette,
> And in the tresorye hyt shette
> Of my brayn, now shal men se
> Yf any vertue in the be
> To tellen al my dream aryght:
> Now kythe thyn engyn and myght!   [HF 523–8

Possibly the phrase, 'kythe thyn engyn', does not amount to
more than 'show your skill'; but the passage has an unusual
interest in attempting to represent the process which brings a
poem into existence. Chaucer seems firmly to reject the idea
that the dream has been impressed on his mind from outside by

some kind of supernatural agency, and asserts that it has been produced by the purposeful workings of his own mental forces. The dream is explicitly described as being created – the verb 'wrot' is from *werchen*, not from *wryten* – by a force or activity which he identifies by the misleading term 'Thought'. The visionary experience wrought by this means is safely contained within his memory, the second of the three medieval sapiences: now is the turn of the third of them, engine, to prove itself by contriving appropriate poetic form and expression for his dream. But 'engyn' does not work independently in this task. When the poet remarks that his readers will discover

> Yf any vertue in the be
> To tellen al my drem aryght: [HF 527–8

he is still addressing 'Thought', which beside bringing the dream into existence is now responsible for telling it, with the help of the 'engyn' which it impels. The sense of the passage cannot be resolved without a proper appreciation of what is involved in 'Thought', which must mean a great deal more than the term suggests to a modern reader. It should not surprise us to discover that imagination and fancy are among its many meanings. The *OED* does not use this passage of Chaucer as an illustration; but the nature and range of the power to which the poet is appealing here leave no doubt of his purpose.

   This is as close as Chaucer ever comes to referring directly to the imagination as Coleridge defined it. The general vagueness of his allusions to this poetically vital subject seem to be explained by the inadequacy of medieval terminology rather than to any imperceptiveness on his part. As we have seen, in its medieval senses the word 'imagination' denoted a much humbler faculty of the mind, not always distinct from fantasy and its merely delusive figures. If 'thought' was indeed the most helpful term available to Chaucer for his purpose in the Proem, we might suppose that current awareness of imagination as a creative force of the mind was rudimentary; and that if imaginative activity was recognised at all it was often confused with much commoner mental functions. With its elementary notions about the workings of the mind, medieval science could hardly be expected to provide any precise classification of mental experiences which, if different in kind, produced much the same impression upon their recipeint; and until the particular nature of each such experience was properly acknowledged the need for a more precise terminology could not be felt. Outside the direct apprehension of substantial reality, all forms of mental impression – whether dream, hallucination, recollection, fantasy or vision – were seen as emanating from a common source in the mind's mysterious ability to present images of absent or non-existent things without regard to fact. Some of these fantasmal creations demanded respect for their fore-shadowing of future events, or for their revelation of divine purposes. The others seemed hardly worth investigating. So far as there was any systematic thinking on the subject, medieval opinion seems to have been much more aware of the suscepti-bility of the mind to false impressions than of its precognitive or visionary powers; and not to have considered it worth while to distinguish between the various kinds of fantasmal experience. We should now regard a dream, with its curious linking together of seemingly unrelated ideas, as differing fundamentally from the creative activity of imagination. To the extent that medieval thinking gave imagination any conscious recognition, it seems not to have admitted that dreams represented a much more arbitrary compilation. The much greater contemporary interest in dreams encouraged the poet to relate his imaginative experiences as if he had dreamt them, and to use conventional figures of the dream-poem to embody his imaginative aware-ness.

In this connection we may find special interest in the figure of the guide or instructor who takes charge of the dreamer and reveals the significance of the strange beings and happenings which he comes across. Macrobius gives no indication how this figure is to be regarded. As Africanus is part of Scipio's dream, it could be assumed that his guide is a creation of his own mind. The prophetic content of the dream discourages this idea, though not enough perhaps to prevent us asking whether a

precognitive power of the mind may be declaring itself through
a form which gives its report a fitting solemnity. The same question about the underlying identity of the prophetic instructor is
raised by one of the simplest of such dreams in Chaucer, where
an intending traveller is warned not to embark:

> Hym thoughte a man stood by his beddes syde,
> And hym comanded that he sholde abyde,
> And seyde hym thus: 'If thou tomorwe wende,
> Thow shalt be dreynt; my tale is at an ende.'
>   [CT VII. 3078–81

The story is characteristically described as 'a greet mervaille',
and perhaps the wonder is increased by the anonymity of the
visitant, whose interest in the sleeper's safety impels the prophesy. If such tales are to be taken seriously – and reports of
such warning dreams are not unknown in our own times – they
suggest that where the mind has precognition of danger, it may
either depict the coming event or describe it in a spoken forecast. In the second case the speaker is seen to be a close relation
of the dreamer or an intimate friend, as though to assure that
the warning will be taken to heart. Where he remains nameless
and mysterious it may be easier to recognise that he represents
the precognitive power of the sleeper himself. At the point of
Scipio's career when his prophetic dream occurred he stood on
the verge of great achievement, where confidence in his final
success was vital to the endeavour he was about to undertake.
The view of the future presented to him by two especially
revered ancestors could be seen as the response of the most
powerful forces of his mind to a momentous challenge. Such
challenges are not altogether unknown in poetry. As Chaucer's
Proem shows, it is a common practice for the writer to invoke
his own creative talents before embarking on a task which will
severely test his abilities. In *The Hous of Fame* the consequences
of the poet's appeal are immediate and startling, for the dreamer
is at once caught up by the great bird who acts as his friendly
instructor during the celestial flight and what follows. In function, though not in manner, the Eagle stands in the same rela-

tionship to the poet-dreamer as Africanus to Scipio in the
Somnium, and we may wonder whether he has the same possible
significance. Within Macrobius' categories the Eagle would be
recognised as the guide or moral teacher of the *oraculum*, from
whom the dreamer learns his fate and the meaning of the
unfamiliar environment to which he is carried. But since *The
Hous of Fame* is a poem rather than a dream, it must be inter-
preted in terms appropriate to poetry, not to dreamlore. The
purposes which Chaucer's reader must try to discern in the
Eagle are imaginative.

It very quickly appears that in respect of size, strength,
understanding and volubility the dreamer is hopelessly out-
matched by his jovial guide, and that the Eagle will not be
content merely with conducting him to the House of Fame. The
bird is a vociferous talker, whose one-sided conversation during
the flight barely allows the dreamer to answer his questions.
Dwarfed and silenced by the enormous creature which has
snatched him up so nonchalantly, the still half-stupefied
dreamer finds that he must submit to a tireless discourse which
after various preliminaries settles into a learned lecture on the
causes and nature of sound. Where the dreamer is timid, hesitant and retiring, the Eagle is a splendidly self-assured figure of
authority who mocks the dreamer's hermit-like existence, and
promises to carry him into the heart of everyday human affairs,
where he will hear every conceivable kind of happening as it
occurs:

> Mo discordes, moo jelousies,
> Mo murmures, and moo novelries,
> And moo dissymulacions,
> And feyned reparacions,
> And moo berdys in two houres
> Withoute rasour or sisoures
> Ymad, then greynes ben of sondes.

[HF 685–91

This sudden expansion of experience will enable the reader to
write at first hand of matters which hitherto he has known only
from books, for in his monkish seclusion he gathers almost

nothing about life. 'Thou hast no tydynges,' the Eagle tells him with patronising amusement,

> 'Of Loves folk yf they be glade,
> Ne of noght elles that God made.'
>
> [HF 645–6

The transformation of this painfully restricted outlook, to be completed by what the dreamer will learn at the end of his journey, begins with the panoramic survey of the world provided by the celestial flight. The initially frightening sensation of being seized and transported by a force of irresistible energy, and the suddenly increased range of vision and perception which accompanies this seizure, are strongly suggestive of the poet's experience as imaginative excitement takes hold of him and impels him towards creation. In two of Chaucer's poems the guide who plucks the dreamer out of seclusion is concerned not merely to enlarge his previously restricted awareness, but to provide matter for a poem which will enable the dreamer to rise above the mediocrity of his past efforts. Africanus seems doubtful whether the dreamer will be able to make use of his remarkable vision, but promises to show him 'mater of to wryte' none the less; and the Eagle explains that

> In som recompensacion
> Of labour and devocion,
> That thou has had, loo, causeles,   [HF 665–7

Jupiter intends to reward the dreamer with 'som maner thing' which in fact becomes the subject of the poem. Like Africanus, the Eagle is an indispensable condition of the experience which the poem describes: without the boisterous guide who takes charge of the dreamer and thrusts him into a world of astonishing figures and events there would be no adventure to describe. The same is true of the poet's imaginative forces, whose working itself provides part of Chaucer's 'mater of to wryte' in these two poems.

Had Chaucer felt impelled to represent his imaginative drive in this way, there is no reason why his dominating *alter ego*

should have appeared only in the dream-poems. The form of the *oraculum* provided a ready means of embodying the state of increased insight and awareness which the poet feels himself to possess at times of creative excitement, in the figure of the ancestor who guides and instructs the awed dreamer. To contrive a counterpart of this impressive being in the poetry of waking life was not impossible; and when Harry Bailly forces the reluctant pilgrim-poet out of hiding, and obliges him to play his part in the entertainment, we recognise the counterpart of Africanus in the world of actual affairs. Like the dreamer in *The Hous of Fame*, this poet is barely conscious of his neighbours, and enjoys only the humblest of talents; and the dominating personality of the Host towers over him with the same good-natured mockery as he finds in the Eagle. The natural authority attributed to the Host in *The General Prologue*, where he is described as fit to be 'a marchal in an halle', is demonstrated by his command of events along the road, and by his shrewd awareness of the tricks and subterfuges of many trades. Beside this paragon of practical wisdom and experience the unworldly poet, timidly offering his wretched 'rym dogerel', is as comic a figure as the bookworm whom the Eagle sets down in the vast concourse of folk thronging the Hall of Fame. However dissimilar the exterior circumstances, in the nature and relationship of the two figures the same conditions persist. The dreamer or pilgrim, to whom Chaucer gives his own name and none of his poetic competence, is a comically reduced version of his true self, evidently designed to contrast forcibly with the figure of confident authority, power, and far-seeing wisdom who takes control of him. The persistence of these linked figures from the dream-poems into Chaucer's final work suggests the vitality of the imaginative concept which they represent.

Images and situations recurring in a poet's work throughout his career give some indication of the underlying form of an imaginative experience which supplies a considerable part of his creative drive. The relationship of the Host to the Canterbury pilgrims seems to embody one such imaginative preoccupation in its finally resolved form. Apart from the

unimpressive narrator of *Sir Thopas*, the pilgrims are a company
of robust, self-willed and highly individual characters whose
energies the Host is not always able to hold in check. The story-
telling competition has hardly started before the Miller challenges the Host's authority by insisting on being heard before
the Monk. His interruption of the orderly sequence which the
Host evidently proposes to observe leads to a further disturbance
when the Miller's tale angers the Reeve; and now the Host must
use his dominating force of character to suppress an explosion
and to ensure that the story-telling continues. Similar challenges
follow as other rivalries emerge, and although the Host's
mastery of his flock is never seriously in question, the task of
guiding and controlling so volatile and dynamic a body taxes
even his resources of strength.

Counterparts of this struggle between an accepted figure of
authority and a noisy, half-rebellious crowd of revellers or
holiday-makers are found in the dream-poems, most obviously
in *The Parlement of Foules*. The great assembly of birds, catalogued by the dreamer much as the narrator of *The Canterbury
Tales* lists and describes his fellow-pilgrims, corresponds to the
company of 'sondry folk' in diversity of character and outlook;
and after behaving decorously during the opening phase of the
debate they too become rowdy and disrespectful. As the situation threatens to get out of hand, Nature asserts herself by telling
the dissidents roughly to hold their tongues, and later by calling
for general silence:

'Now pes,' quod Nature, 'I comaunde heer!'   [PF 617

Although unlike in many superficial ways, the basic likeness of
the two situations would not be contested. In both, a lively and
noisily animated crowd, at first restrained by respect for order
and the importance of the occasion, agrees to take part in a
form of discussion where each individual contributes, beginning
with the highest in rank. After the courtly opinion has been
expressed at some length, the plebeian members of the group
grow impatient and restless; and a threat of open dispute is only
averted when the figure of authority intervenes and imposes its

own settlement on the debate. In his final work Chaucer did
not reach the point at which the Host, as 'juge and reportour',
gives his opinion of the tales which he has invited; but the
conditions outlined by the Host before the pilgrims leave the
Tabard indicate the poet's intentions plainly enough, and show
how the parallel was to complete itself.

At first sight neither *The Boke of the Duchesse* nor *The Hous of
Fame* appears to duplicate this concern with a contest between
authority and disorder; but both poems contain signs that
Chaucer was feeling his way towards expression of this emerging
interest. Of the two great crowds of people whom the dreamer
meets in *The Hous of Fame*, the numberless 'congregacioun of
folk' inside the House of Rumour is suggestively akin to Chaucer's later companies of unruly birds and pilgrims, and not only
in the inclusion of pilgrims, shipmen and pardoners among its
ceaselessly gossiping occupants. Like the plebeian birds of *The
Parlement of Foules*, and still more like their counterparts among
the Canterbury pilgrims, these talkers are noisy and undisciplined; not speaking in turn but gabbling news and hearsay in
an unbroken outpouring of sound:

> 'Thus hath he sayd', and 'Thus he doth',
> 'Thus shal hit be', 'Thus herde y seye',
> 'That shal be founde', 'That dar I leye'. [HF 2052–4

But unlike the birds of the other poem, this crowd lacks a figure
who might impose order upon its confused and undirected
activity. The narrative breaks off, in fact, at the point where
such a figure, an unidentified 'man of gret auctorite', has just
entered the building as if in answer to this implicit need; but the
interruption of the story leaves Chaucer's purpose uncertain. If
the mysterious character whom the dreamer glimpses over the
heads of the excited crowd is imaginatively related to the figures
of authority in other poems, his significance must be looked for
in Chaucer's creative impulse, and not in contemporary social
history. The same is probably true of the unseen 'emperour
Octovien' said to be leading the great hunt which the dreamer
joins in *The Boke of the Duchesse*. The 'gret route'

> Of huntes and eke of foresteres,
> With many relayes and lymeres   [BD 361–2

which sweeps the dreamer towards the forest seems to be an early counterpart of the other predominantly lower-class gatherings, and like the crowd in the House of Rumour they have no dominating figure to direct them. The dreamer's eagerness to catch up with the emperor, shown by his excited response to the news the Octovien is close by –

> 'A Goddes half, in good tyme!' quod I,
> 'Go we faste!' and gan to ryde   [BD 370–1

– matches the impatience of the mob in the House of Rumour to see the great man who is about to enter their hall:

> For I saugh rennynge every wight,
> As faste as that they hadden myght . . .
> And whan they were alle on an hepe,
> Tho behynde begunne up lepe,
> And clamben up on other faste.
>
> [HF 2145–51

They are more fortunate than the first of Chaucer's dreamers, who fails to obtain even a fleeting glimpse of Octovien.

The incident is a minor feature of *The Boke of the Duchesse*, but it may be the first expression of an imaginative impulse in Chaucer which cannot become intelligible until it is seen fully developed in his later work. In this first handling of the dream-poem Chaucer raises the expectation that a figure 'of gret auctorite' will appear, but Octovien remains an allusion. At the end of Chaucer's next poem such a figure does arrive, as though to take control of the incoherent activity inside the spinning House of Rumour; but the narrative goes no further. In *The Parlement of Foules* Chaucer seems to come much closer to a realisation of his imaginative concern, for now the figure of authority is firmly installed, and maintains a rule of order over her angrily disputing subjects. In his final poem Chaucer transfers the representative of authority from dream-world to waking life, without modifying the now familiar pattern of ideas.

The Host who already has the power of a commanding personality, is granted special powers by the pilgrims which supplement this innate authority. They agree to regard him as their 'governour', and to submit to him 'at his devys' without respect to their social standing. The churls, and some others who occasionally forget this agreement, display the same noisy ebullience and discourtesy as their counterparts in *The Parlement of Foules*, and are checked with the same outspoken bluntness.

Whatever the final significance of this recurrent motif in Chaucer's work, he seems to be pursuing the same imaginative end in the dream-poems as elsewhere, without modifying his purposes out of respect for different literary genres. The meaning of the dream-poems must be sought in those features of his writing which represent imaginative activity generally. We understand a poem when we realise what it embodies of the writer's inward experience, not when we have matched its figures and happenings against a set of corresponding characters and events drawn from actual life. It does not explain *The Boke of the Duchesse* as a poem to suppose that the Man in Black stands for John of Gaunt, or *The Parlement of Foules* if we regard the formel eagle as personifying Anne of Bohemia. To the contrary, by refusing to admit that the inner meaning of a poem is imaginative we make interpretation more difficult by confusing the nature of its task. The happening represented by *The Boke of the Duchesse* has no counterpart or equivalent in other kinds of experience, and the poem must be treated as the record of a unique event whose primary significance was for Chaucer himself. The dreamer's adventure, both before and after he falls asleep, resembles a dream in being made up of incidents and figures taken from the poet's imaginative stock, and shaped into a complex occurrence which gives form to his awareness of himself and his private world of ideas. Taken together, the three poems discussed in this book enable us to grasp something of that imaginative world and to reach a limited understanding of the private concerns which Chaucer pursues and presents to himself through the dreamer's experience.

II

THE BOKE OF THE DUCHESSE

In each of Chaucer's dream-poems the dreamer's experience falls into two parts, concerned respectively with his sleeping and waking lives. The story begins with some account of his waking activities and preoccupations during the day leading up to his dream; a prelude which serves both to introduce him and to indicate motifs which may be picked up and developed in what follows, as he falls asleep. By this means the two parts of his experience may be drawn more closely together than their very different natures might initially suggest, for although the dreamer is carried well beyond the normal range of his awareness, the particular interests of his dream may be foreshadowed in his ruminations or his reading immediately before falling asleep. A student of Macrobius might regard such a dream as a mere *insomnium*, which takes over the concerns of the waking mind; but in the context of imaginative writing such a prefiguring of the poet's later subject-matter has a different significance. The dream is in fact part of a poem whose ideas are repeated and developed as part of the familiar process which gives it unity. Here it is not the associative linking of the *insomnium* which brings together sleeping and waking experience, but the working of an imaginative force which impresses a single design upon the whole of the dreamer's adventure.

In *The Boke of the Duchesse* the dreamer's waking experience takes up a greater part of the story than in either of the two other dream-poems, and also runs to a greater length, amounting to nearly three hundred lines. The dreamer has an excuse for taking such an unconscionable time to fall asleep, for he is suffering from insomnia so badly that he feels his life to be in danger. 'I have gret wonder, be this lyght,' he begins his story,

How that I lyve, for day ne nyght
I may nat slepe wel nygh noght.   [BD 2–3

This traditional gambit, which Chaucer had encountered in
Machaut and Froissart, makes the delay in coming to the
dream plausible in terms of story, but it does not explain why
Chaucer spent so long on the introductory section of his poem.
The length of this waking passage suggests that he found much
to attract him imaginatively in the prelude to the dream, and
was not impatient to have the dreamer fall asleep. It might be
mistaken, then, to suppose that this poem is simply about the
dream, and that the lively introduction is a mere narrative
preliminary to the encounter in the forest and the mourning
knight's story. A proper understanding of the poem requires us
to give equally attentive reading to both parts of the dreamer's
tale, and to be alert for relationships between them; taking
nothing for granted, and in particular resisting the view that
The Boke of the Duchesse is imaginatively accountable as a courtly
elegy on the death of Blanche. There is no cause to quarrel with
the traditional belief that John of Gaunt's bereavement in 1369
provided the historical occasion of the poem, for this is supported both by internal references and by the more explicit title
which Chaucer gives this work in his *Legend of Good Women*:

He made the bok that highte the Hous of Fame,
And ek the Deth of Blaunche the Duchesse.
                              [LGW G.405–6

But to be successful a poem must satisfy an inner compulsion,
which although possibly triggered by an historical event is
unlikely to derive its energies entirely from that source. However closely *The Boke of the Duchesse* accommodates itself to the
courtly obligation which the death of Blanche placed on
Chaucer, the primary task of the poem is to give form to its
author's private awareness; and even a cursory reading of *The
Boke of the Duchesse* shows that its concern with the dead lady is
only one of many issues, some of them incompatible with an
elegaic purpose. Though not so lengthy a preamble as the Wife
of Bath's audience must submit to, the preliminaries to the

dreamer's meeting with the Man in Black show Chaucer fully
occupied with a wide variety of topics, and in no hurry to pro-
ceed. When the narrative is taken over by this new character,
the poem loses its diversity of interest and undergoes a fundamental change of mood. If we regard the Man in Black's story
as the dominating element of the poem, we are left to explain
the function of its opening four hundred and fifty lines, and to
suggest how the waking section and the first episodes of the
dream are to be fitted into a reading of the whole work.

In beginning the poem with a reference to the dreamer's
'defaute of slep' Chaucer may be borrowing from Froissart, but
he is also introducing a theme which persists in a variety of
forms throughout the waking section of the story. In the opening forty-five lines there are seven allusions to the narrator's
sleeplessness, and an admission that his life is threatened by the
physical exhaustion which his insomnia produces:

> For nature wolde nat suffyse
> To noon erthly creature
> Nat longe tyme to endure
> Without slep and be in sorwe.   [BD 18–21

To ask why he cannot sleep is a waste of effort, for the victim
himself cannot understand or explain his weariness and depression; though he hints at a love-sickness suffered 'this eight yeer'
and at the particular physician who alone might cure him.
With this muted indication of his private trouble the dreamer
brightens a little, and decides to while away the night by reading. The book which comes into his hands is a collection of tales,
and the story which he lights upon proves relevant to his own
unhappy condition. It tells how, after the death of Seys at sea,
his wife Alcyone is unable to bear her uncertainty about his
fate, and begs Juno to send her enlightenment through a
dream:

> Send me grace to slepe, and mete
> In my slep som certeyn sweven
> Wherthourgh that I may knowen even
> Whether my lord be quyk or ded.
>
> [BD 118–21

Alcyone's distress associates her with the dreamer, who also
hopes to find relief from despondency in sleep, and perhaps the
answer to the unresolved problem which keeps him awake.
When Alcyone faints from exhaustion, 'forweped and forwaked',
she is put to bed by her women; and there she falls into a profound sleep 'or that she tooke kep', as Juno grants her request.
The goddess then sends a messenger to Morpheus, ordering him
to take Seys' drowned body from the sea and display it to the
sleeping queen as a still living figure, from whom Alcyone will
learn the truth:

> And do the body speke ryght soo,
> Ryght as hyt was woned to doo
> The whiles that hit was alyve.   [BD 149–51

The notion that Seys' body must be brought to the bedside to
induce a prophetic dream seems curiously alien to medieval
thinking on the subject, and does not appear in Ovid's version
of the myth which Chaucer was using. But similar corpse-like
figures in *The Boke of the Duchesse* might lead us to guess that this
ghastly physical revenant, 'ful pale and nothyng rody', has a
purposeful place in Chaucer's design. Some of its counterparts
are described when the story moves with Juno's messenger to
the dark valley where Morpheus and his inert subjects lie
paralysed by sleep. In Ovid's version of the story the region is
characterised by its complete silence. 'No wild beasts are heard,
no cattle, nor is there any sound of branches swaying in the
wind, nor harsh quarrelling of human tongues.'[1] Chaucer
ignores this point, and depicts Morpheus' kingdom as an
unproductive wasteland:

> Ther never yet grew corn ne gras,
> Ne tre, ne nothing that ought was,
> Beste, ne man, ne noght elles,
> Save ther were a fewe welles
> Came rennynge fro the clyves adoun,
> That made a dedly slepynge soun.
>
> [BD 157–62

---

[1] *The Metamorphoses*, tr. M.M. Innes, London 1955; p. 285.

At the bottom of the valley, in the darkest cave, lie Morpheus and his son, 'that slep and dide noon other werk'; surrounded by sleepers whose attitudes suggest not fatigue so much as self-abandonment and spiritual defeat:

> Somme henge her chyn upon hir brest,
> And slept upryght, her hed yhed,
> And somme lay naked in her bed
> And slepe whiles the dayes laste.
>
> [BD 174–7

The phrase 'whiles the dayes laste' carries a perceptible hint of moral disapproval at the sleepers' wasting of time; a hint made easier to catch by Chaucer's picture of the sterile landscape about the cave. This critical attitude, and the general impression of dejected lethargy conveyed by the sleepers, stand in ironic contrast to Alcyone's plea for 'grace to slepe', and still more with the dreamer's fear that he may die of insomnia. Where they both have an almost desperate need of sleep, seeing it as the only cure for the crushing depression which weighs upon them, the sleepers in Morpheus' cave appear so completely overcome by apathy that they have lost all capacity for constructive action. The same state of being is used to represent both health and sickness, restoration and self-annihilation.

The implicit danger that sleep may deepen into senseless inertia seems to be recognised in the noisy efforts of Juno's messenger to rouse Morpheus and his companions to an awareness of waking reality. In Ovid's version of the tale the message is delivered by Iris, who wakes Morpheus silently by the radiance of her garments, which flood the cave with light. Chaucer substitutes for the goddess a brisk and unceremonious mortal figure, and creates for himself an early opportunity to indulge a talent for lively colloquial dialogue. He also gives the episode a sense of strenuous urgency which he did not find in the *Metamorphoses*:

> This messager com fleynge faste
> And cried, 'O ho! awake anoon!'
> Hit was for noght; ther herde hym non.

'Awake!' quod he, 'whoo ys lyth there?'
And blew his horn ryght in here eere,
And cried 'Awaketh!' wonder hye.
This god of slep with hys oon ye
Cast up, axed, 'Who clepeth there?'
'Hyt am I,' quod this messager.   [BD 178–86

The comic energy of the passage does not entirely disguise the
gravity of a situation, where the sleepers are sunk in a lethargy
so profound that not even the blast of a horn can disturb them.
Chaucer's modifications of the original story seem designed to
underline a significance which he reads into Ovid's tale, and
which could not be represented by its much quieter tone. The
noisy invasion of Sleep's kingdom by a messenger who embodies
the energies of common life transforms Ovid's account of the
waking of Morpheus, concentrating its interest upon the
messenger's clamorous efforts to rouse sleepers drowned in
oblivion. Their dejected attitudes suggest that these are not
ordinary sleepers, but men crushed by a melancholy so intense
that nothing can break in upon their stupefied misery.

Such a desolation of spirit, which destroys the will to partici-
pate in the common business of life, takes possession of Alcyone;
and the spectral figure which brings her the certainty of Seys'
death shows the danger of her depression by trying to arouse
her to awareness of the futility of grief. 'My swete wyf,' he tells
her, with a husband's concern for her well-being,

'Awake! let be your sorwful lyf!
For in your sorwe there lyth no red.
For certes, swete, I nam but ded:
Ye shul me never on lyve yse.'   [BD 202–5

His advice seems unsympathetically practical: Alcyone must
accept the fact that Seys is dead and that lamentation will not
bring him back. Unlike Ovid's Ceyx, who concludes his message
by reminding Alcyone of her duty to mourn her lost husband –
'Do not send me unwept into the void of Tartarus' – Chaucer's
revenant wishes her to spare herself the distress and exhaustion
of unrestrained grief. This attitude is implicit in his peremptory

command, 'Awake!' which Alcyone must obviously not obey literally, since she can only hear his revelation if she continues to sleep. The implications of 'Awake!' are seen in his advice to Alcyone to put aside her grieving, which can do no good: she must wake up to the painful realities of life, and accept them. The good sense of this counsel is plainly demonstrated when Alcyone ignores the rebuke and abandons herself to sorrow, for she dies within three days: a development which Chaucer did not take from Ovid, whose Alcyone is metamorphosed into a sea-bird after discovering her husband's body on the shore. Her metamorphosis must be irrelevant to Chaucer's purposes, for the dreamer ends his recapitulation of the myth by remarking that the rest of the tale concerns what Alcyone 'sayede more in that swow', which would take too long to repeat.[1]

Earlier, the dreamer has declared that the story of Alcyone's grief affected him so deeply that he 'ferde the worse al the morwe': an appropriately courtly remark response to a pathetic tale, but not a remark to treat seriously. His interest in Alcyone is soon to be replaced by a much greater absorption in the melancholy figure whom he meets in his dream; and even before this encounter the dreamer is much more intrigued by the idea of appealing to Morpheus than of evoking sympathy for Alcyone. Without apparently noticing the note of moral censure which her story has been made to carry, he returns to the problem of his sleeplessness; though now in a much lighter spirit. Adopting a more familiar mode of address, he admits how astonished he is to learn of beings who could control men's sleeping:

> For I had never herd speke, or tho,
> Of noo goddes that koude make
> Men to slepe, ne for to wake.   [BD 234–6

But seizing the offered remedy, he resolves to secure the help of whatever god may be able to save him from dying of insomnia:

---

[1] His counterpart in *The Hous of Fame* gives the same excuse for not providing a full account of Dido's speech before committing suicide: see HF 376–82.

Rather then that y shulde deye
Thorgh defaute of slepynge thus,
I wolde yive thilke Morpheus,
Or hys goddesse, dame Juno,
Or som wight elles, I ne roghte who,
To make me slepe and have some reste –
I wil yive hym the alderbeste
Yifte that ever he abod hys lyve.

[BD 240–7

The comic ignorance which allows the dreamer to mistake Juno
for Morpheus' wife, and the colloquial manner of the whole
passage, indicate a surprising shift of attitude in Chaucer. The
narrator speaks of feeling 'such pitee and such rowthe' at
Alcyone's story, as though indicating the reaction expected of
his readers; but the jocular spirit of his attempt to bribe
Morpheus 'or som wight elles' with a handsome present
destroys this impression. The dreamer, no longer well-read but
entirely unacquainted with mythology, has been transformed
from a listless victim of despondency into an affably talkative
figure who is willing to try any remedy, however implausible, for
the insomnia which he now treats as a joke. As though un-
affected by the pitiful tale he has just read, he comes near to
parodying Alcyone's plea to Juno by offering the god of sleep a
luxuriously comfortable feather-bed in exchange for a good
night's rest. 'Yif he wol make me slepe a lyte,' he promises,

Of down of pure dowves white
I wil yive hym a fether-bed,
Rayed with gold, and ryght wel cled
In fyn blak satyn doutremer,
And many a pilowe, and every ber
Of cloth of Reynes, to slepe softe:
Hym thar not nede to turnen ofte.   [BD 250–6

The speaker's practical interest in design and materials, and the
heavy witticism of his final remark, show how much his previously courtly position has been eroded. From the leisured
environment which provides him with attendants to bring him
books he has descended to a humbler social level represented by

his involvement with bedding and pillow-cases, and by the idiomatic liveliness of his language. The comedy of lines 221–269 depends mainly on the dreamer's incongruously practical approach to Morpheus, whom he addresses with disarming familiarity. 'This ylke god, Morpheus,' he concludes amiably, determined to strike a fair bargain,

> May wynne of me moo fees thus
> Than ever he wan; and to Juno
> That ys hys goddesse, I shal soo do,
> I trow that she shal holde hir payd.   [BD 266–9]

Where Chaucer follows his own narrative line the courtly figure dissolves, and a characteristic impulse of comedy colours the writing. The dreamer who hopes to tempt the god with a solidly material reward has the well-meaning ignorance which Chaucer gives to other narrators; but in *The Boke of the Duchesse* this comic quality is at odds with the initial sombreness of mood, and the more prolonged melancholy of the story which the dreamer is to hear. In consequence the narrative centre shifts between two viewpoints: one respectful towards courtly attitudes and conventions, the other adopting the commonsense standards of everyday life, often comic in themselves and frequently inviting amusement by their remoteness from aristocratic ideals. The splendid bed offered to Morpheus, with its black satin 'doutremer' and Breton linen, stands in the poem as an emblem of its central theme; representing both the comfort brought by sleep and the state of spiritual torpor threatening those who abandon themselves to despondency. Like Alcyone and the bereaved Man in Black whom he will later meet, the dreamer declares himself oppressed by 'sorwful ymagynacioun'; and in looking for sleep he may be encouraging himself to become as inert and unhearing as the unresponsive figures in Morpheus' cave. But the bed also symbolises dreaming, and the better understanding which he may acquire through the fantasmal experience which at this point of the poem is about to start.

Paradoxically, it begins with waking. The dreamer's offer is

hardly out of his mouth before Morpheus, as though unable to
resist such an inducement, puts him to sleep over his open book,
and at once the dream commences. 'Me thoughte thus,' the
dreamer explains,

> that hyt was May,
> And in the dawenynge I lay –
> Me mette thus – in my bed al naked,
> And loked forth, for I was waked
> With smale foules a gret hep
> That had affrayed me out of my slep,
> Thorgh noyse and swetnesse of her song.   [BD 291–7

Hitherto in the story the impulse embodied in the command
'Awake!' has been frustrated, first by a drugged unconsciousness
of the outside world, and then by the grief which saps Alcyone's
will to survive her personal tragedy; but now a dreamer is
successfully roused from sleep by a great chorus of birdsong on a
May morning. In fact he has not woken at all, but fallen asleep;
but the effect of this paradoxical opening to the dream is to
suggest that this 'waking' is the true event, and a release from
illusion. The state of mind described in the opening lines of the
poem, in which the dreamer feels nothing but a stunned sense
of desolation, instantly gives way to pleasure and exhilaration
as he wakes to bright sunlight, a richly decorated bedchamber
and the cheerful singing of birds on the tiles overhead:

> So mery a soun, so swete entewnes,
> That certes, for the toun of Tewnes,
> I nolde but I had herd hem synge;
> For al my chambre gan to rynge
> Thurgh syngynge of her armonye.
>
> [BD 309–13

The dreamer has woken into a world of joyful activity and
excitement, where the birds sing with unrestrained exuberance,
nature and art together displaying their greatest brilliance and
colour. His pleasure at the 'mery crafty notes' of the birds is
heightened as he studies the painted walls and windows of his
room, and recognises – with the help of his courtly *persona* –

some of the celebrated figures of the Trojan War, and illustrations of scenes in the *Roman de la Rose*. A warm and cloudless
morning adds to his delight, as sunlight streams through the
windows upon his bed:

> And eke the welken was so fair:
> Blew, bryght, clere was the ayr,
> And ful attempre for sothe hyt was;
> For nother to cold nor hoot yt nas,
> Ne in al the welken was no clowde.

[BD 339–43

The cloudless sky suggests how far behind the dreamer has left
the storm and its wrecking of Alcyone's happiness; a disaster
with which his own sleeplessness has associated him. For a
moment he lies inactive, marvelling at the vitality of life about
him; but he is soon challenged to exchange his bed for the
vigorous exertions of the hunt:

> And as I lay thus, wonder lowde
> Me thoght I herde a hunte blowe
> T'assay hys horn, and for to knowe
> Whether hyt were clere or hors of soun.
> And I herde goynge, bothe up and doun,
> Men, hors, houndes, and other thyng;
> And al men speken of huntyng.

[BD 344–50

The tentative blast on the horn might be an echo from the
previous phase of the dreamer's experience, from which he is
now decisively separated. It may also have some significance for
the young Chaucer, who is now to discover whether his creative
gift is great enough to produce an original poem, embodying
his own outlook and ideas. But primarily the muted horn-blast
represents a challenge to the dreamer to shake off his torpor
and commit himself to the world of affairs – 'men, hors, houndes,
and other thyng' – which hitherto he has ignored by retiring
into a book. Self-isolated by the melancholy which made him
'tak no kep of nothyng', he has been cut off from purposeful
occupation: now, like the sleepers in Morpheus' cave, he has an

opportunity to throw off his lassitude and immerse himself in a wide-awake course of action. Unlike those other dreamers, who 'slepe whiles the dayes laste', he leaps from his bed to answer the huntsman's summons. 'When I herde that,' he comments,

> I was ryght glad, and up anoon
> Took my hors, and forth I wente
> Out of my chambre; I never stente
> Til I com to the feld withoute.
> Ther overtok I a gret route
> Of huntes and eke of foresteres,
> With many relayes and lymeres,
> And hyed hem to the forest faste,
> And I with hem. [BD 356–64

The passage begins with a sense of dreamlike insubstantiality as the horse appears before the dreamer has left his bedchamber; but the impression of energy and rapid movement, and the sudden widening of physical boundaries as the dreamer gallops towards open country, are the reverse of dreamlike. He has rejected inertia and solitude for the headlong pursuit which carries him towards the great concourse of hunters and foresters, surging after the yet unseen leader of the hunt. Nothing in his behaviour or outlook now suggests that he is sleeping; and the excited urgency of the passage is markedly unlike the contemplative stillness of most dream-poems, whose figures and settings have the motionless charm of works of art. A snatch of conversation between the dreamer and one of the kennelmen gives fresh impetus to his eager spurring forward. 'Say, felowe, who shal hunte here?' he shouts, in a question which has the ring of everyday speech; and hearing that the emperor Octovien is leading the cavalcade, he redoubles his efforts to reach the foremost riders:

> 'A Goddes half, in good tyme!' quod I,
> 'Go we faste!' [BD 370–1

Again the speaker's colloquial energy and directness associate him with waking life and affairs, not with the remoteness and delicacy of a courtly vision; but the forward rush of the poem is

about to slacken. As the hunt reaches the fringes of the forest the
master-huntsman

> anoon, fot-hot,
> With a gret horn blew thre mot   [BD 375–6

to signal that the hounds have been uncoupled. Although the
emphasis of 'anoon, fot-hot' maintains the impression of haste,
and the great horn repeats its stirring challenge, the promise of
a culmination of excitement is disappointed. The hart eludes its
pursuers, and the chase peters out in a sense of dejection that is
almost literally admitted when the master-huntsman sounds 'a
forloyn at the laste'.

A much quieter passage follows. Its opening words, 'I was go
walked fro my tree', show the dreamer out of the saddle and no
longer strenuously active, but now shaping towards the mysterious experience which forms the main substance of his dream.
A young hound, separated from the pack, approaches the
dreamer as though it knew him, but slips away into the depths
of the forest when he tries to seize it:

> I wolde have kaught hyt, and anoon
> Hyt fledde, and was fro me goon.   [BD 395–6

This unexplained incident, dreamlike in its oddity, represents a
return by Chaucer to the traditions of the love-vision; and is in
fact modelled upon the dreamer's encounter with a more imposing animal in Machaut's *Dit dou Lyon*. The submissive behaviour
of Machaut's lion, who approaches the dreamer

> aussi humblement
> Com se fust un petit chiennet   [DL 326–7

has obviously provided the pattern for Chaucer's whelp, even to
the detail described a few lines later, when the lion allows the
dreamer to stroke him, 'et joint les oreilles'. Chaucer also copies
Machaut in making the creature act as guide to the dreamer,
though in a much less formal way; for in chasing the whelp
through the forest the dreamer comes across the Man in Black
as though by hazard. As this pursuit takes him through a glade

covered with flowers and soft grass, the dreamer loses contact
with the absorbing physical activities of Octovien's hunt and
passes into a purely fictional world, familiar to medieval readers
as the setting of the *Roman de la Rose* and a score of derivative
poems. To express his delight at the beauty of the scene the
dreamer reassumes his literate character, remarking that

> both Flora and Zephirus,
> They two that make floures growe,
> Had mad her dwellynge ther, I trowe.
>
> [BD 403–4

Great trees 'of fourty or fifty fadme lengthe' canopy the ground,
providing shade for animals of every kind, so numerous that not
even Argus, 'the noble countour', could have reckoned them all.
By re-establishing the dreamer's courtly identity this second
mythological reference shows that Chaucer has again shifted
his imaginative standpoint from waking experience to the conventional ground of a visionary ideal. At this stage of the poem
the dream proper is about to begin, after some four hundred
lines and a series of events in which waking reality and illusion
are not always clearly distinguished, and varying in character
between pathos and outright farce, as though the poet found it
difficult to commit himself unambiguously to his serious courtly
theme.

The rest of the poem has no such uncertainty of purpose, and
much less variety of subject-matter and tone. The next nine
hundred lines are dominated by the Man in Black's story, into
which the dreamer intrudes only occasionally as he questions
the speaker or urges him to throw off his deadly melancholy.
These short exchanges give the poem an element of tension, for
although the dreamer sympathises with the knight's abject
misery he also recognises the danger of his self-abandoning grief,
and protests energetically at such a wilful prolonging of sorrow.
But these objections are too short and infrequent to form an
effective counterpoise to the Man in Black's emotional extremism; and the main impression left by this long passage is of the
knight's inconsolable grief, not of the dreamer's matter-of-fact

protests. Their meeting involves several characteristic circumstances and incidents of the courtly vision, one at least lifted
from Machaut without acknowledgement. In his *Jugement dou
Roy de Behaingne* the French poet describes a similar encounter,
between a dreamer and a lady too preoccupied with sorrow to
be immediately aware of his presence, who then apologises for
her apparent lack of politeness:

> 'Certes, sire, pas ne vous entendi
> Pour mon penser que le me deffendi;
>   Mais se j'ay fait
> Riens ou il ait villenie ou meffait,
> Vueilliez le moy pardonner, s'il vous plait.' [RB 70–74

Chaucer justifies his borrowing of the incident by preparing us
for the dazed unresponsiveness of the Man in Black, who cannot
at first be aroused by the newcomer, through the parallel
incident in Morpheus' cave. The knight's dejected attitude as
he 'heng hys hed adoun' should remind us of the frozen figures
who slept 'upryght, hir hed yhed', heedless of passing time.
Although not literally asleep, the Man in Black is too blind to
everything but his grief to notice the dreamer's arrival. 'I went
and stood ryght at his fet,' the dreamer relates,

> And grette hym, but he spak noght,
> But argued with his owne thoght,
> And in hys wyt disputed faste
> Why and how hys lyf myght laste.[1]   [BD 503–6

Unconscious of the world about him, the Man in Black shares
the condition of the sleepers described in the myth, and like them
he needs to be shaken out of a dangerous trance. Later, when
the dreamer appreciates the seriousness of this threat, he
attempts to wake the Man in Black to a sense of his peril by a
rebuke as outspoken and uncourtly as the trumpet-blast which

---

[1] The dreamer cannot know what the Man in Black is thinking: if he
could read his thoughts there would be no long delay in learning the
cause of the knight's profound depression. Evidently Chaucer allows him
to step out of character briefly, for the sake of the reader's better understanding. This passage deserves to be remembered during arguments
about the dreamer's ignorance of the bereavement admitted in lines
477–84.

Juno's messenger blows directly into the sleepers' ears; but at their first exchange the dreamer speaks with the politeness and consideration of gentle manners. The apology which he offers in return implies the same background of good breeding:

> 'I am ryght sory yif I have ought
> Destroubled yow out of your thought.
> Foryive me, yif I have mystake.'   [BD 523–5

This suggestion of social kinship is not the only link between the two characters. The mental depression which paralyses the Man in Black is an aggravated form of the listless melancholy which weighs down the dreamer at the beginning of his story. It is evidently because Chaucer wishes to develop the original idea of dazed inertness that he allows the dreamer to look into the knight's mind and to diagnose a state of suicidal despair closely similar to his own earlier condition, when he felt astonished at remaining alive despite the exhaustion of his sleeplessness. Now, apparently cured of his own depression by a combination of waking and sleeping experience, he describes another victim of the same self-defeating melancholy:

> Hit was gret wonder that Nature
> Myght suffre any creature
> To have such sorwe, and be not ded.

>   [BD 467–9

The parallel might mean only that Chaucer is giving each figure the same formal introduction; suggesting – with help from Froissart or Machaut – that both are desolate lovers for whom the reader must feel sympathy and respect. But the first of the two figures has now thrown off his initial depression, and his comic appeal to Morpheus has suggested an uncourtly readiness to joke at his previously desperate state of mind. The reader is now brought back to this pathetic ideal by a narrator who has meanwhile exchanged his original manner and outlook for a position which accepts a more workaday standard of behaviour. His practical sense begins to prove itself when the dreamer encourages the Man in Black to unburden himself by revealing the cause of his grief. 'Certes, sire,' he proposes,

> 'yif that yee
> Wolde ought discure me youre woo,
> I wolde, as wys God helpe me soo,
> Amende hyt, yif I kan or may.'
>
> [BD 548–51

The dream is providing a means of externalising the dreamer's uncomprehended misery in waking life, and of rationalising its effects upon a second victim.

In another respect the relationship of the two characters is less easily determined. Before the Man in Black becomes aware of the dreamer's presence, he either sings or recites a complaint, 'of rym ten vers or twelve', which leaves no doubt about the cause of his desolation:

> 'I have of sorwe so gret won
> That joye gete I never non,
> Now that I see my lady bryght,
> Which I have loved with al my myght,
> Is fro me ded and ys agoon.'   [BD 475–9

Since this is not intended for the dreamer's ears, it could be politeness that makes him speak later as though he had no inkling of the loss the knight has suffered. If the dreamer does indeed realise the reason for the Man in Black's misery, some of his remarks will seem unthinkably harsh and unfeeling. We could suppose that despite having heard the knight refer explicitly to his lady's death, the dreamer fails to take the point, and blunders along the well-meaning course which ends in astonishment when he forces the Man of Black to declare the plain fact, 'She ys ded!' which nothing else could bring home to him. If the dreamer is merely pretending to be astonished by the disclosure, the poem itself must lose something by the discrediting of its climax. His overhearing of the knight's lament creates an obvious difficulty unless, as in lines 504–6, Chaucer is making use of him to supply information needed by the reader, which in his narrative character the dreamer does not share. If he does indeed hear the lament, two circumstances might explain why he fails to recognise its significance. First, like the narrator in the

two subsequent dream-poems, he is not remarkably bright, and
may need to have relatively simple facts spelled out to him. His
slow-wittedness does not always appear, for just as sometimes he
shows himself well-read and cultured, so too he sometimes
reverses the impression of his comic ignorance by speaking with
dignity and sensitive feeling. It does not seem possible to recon-
cile these conflicting impressions of the dreamer. When he
tries to engage the Man in Black in small talk, in the hope of
reaching some understanding of his trouble, both his strategy
and his conversation suggest the sophisticated manners of a
courtier:

> 'Sir,' quod I, 'this game is doon.
> I holde that this hert be goon;
> These huntes konne hym nowher see.'
>
> [BD 539–41

His remark conforms with the picture which the dreamer gives
of himself by his preference of a book to 'ches or tables', by his
appreciation of the painted bedchamber, and by his eagerness
to join the royal hunt: an habitué of the court, at home with its
characteristic sports and diversions, and with a developed taste
for literature and the arts. The cheerfully garrulous dreamer
who tries to bribe Morpheus with the finest present 'that ever
he abod hys lyve' comes from another world, as does the speaker
who supposes that the knight is suicidally depressed over a lost
chess-piece:

> 'But ther is no man alyve her
> Wolde for a fers make this woo!' [BD 740–1

Chaucer's purpose seems to be divided between a traditional
conception of the dreamer as a sensitive and discerning figure of
courtly life, and a comic impulse struggling to find expression
through the same figure. The dreamer of *The Boke of the
Duchesse* is consequently an odd combination of two incompatible characters, differing in temperament and social status;
one widely read in mythology and courtly romance, the other
unfamiliar with fiction of any kind, and most at home in the

atmosphere of bourgeois practicality and good sense, where the other is in close touch with the standard of courtly manners and judgement. Even had the dreamer not overheard the knight's lament for his dead mistress, what he sees of the lover's profound grief should make it impossible to misinterpret the cause of his despair. But the dreamer is evidently too much a stranger to the Man in Black's world of romantic extremism to recognise the implications of his abject state of mind; and his blindness demands the long explanation which takes up the greater part of Chaucer's poem.

The Man in Black's story, describing his wooing and eventual acceptance as a lover, follows literary convention very closely and presents no surprises to a reader familiar with the traditions of *fine amour*. It could hardly be otherwise, for Chaucer is borrowing extensively from Machaut; particularly from his *Remede de Fortune* and the *Jugement dou Roy de Behaingne*.[1] The description of 'goode faire White' which takes up lines 816–1040 draws extensively upon the *Roy de Behaingne*, with some help from the *Remede de Fortune*; and the same two poems provide most of the substance of lines 1180–312, which conclude the knight's story. All the typical elements of a tale of courtly love process before us. The lover is young, and already dedicated to an ideal of love, though as yet he is without experience, Unable to devote himself to any other interest or undertaking, he chooses love as his 'firste craft' in preference to other possible accomplishments:

> For that tyme Yowthe, my maistresse,
> Governed me in ydelnesse;
> For hyt was in my firste youthe,
> And thoo ful lytel good y couthe,
> For al my werkes were flyttynge
> That tyme, and al my thoght varyinge.[2]
>
> [BD 797–802

[1] Robinson notes that the knight's outburst against Fortune in lines 617–709 draws upon at least four of Machaut's poems.

[2] Closely based on Machaut: 'Que juenesse me gouvernoit/Et en oiseuse me tenoit,/ Mes ouevres estoient volages:/Varians estoit mes corages.' – *Remede de Fortune*, 47–50.

The missing focus of attention is suddenly provided for him when he comes upon a group of beautiful women, of whom one so dazzles him by her outstanding charm and attractiveness that he surrenders himself to her immediately:

> That she ful sone, in my thoght,
> As helpe me God, so was ykaught
> So sodenly, that I ne tok
> No maner conseyl but at hir lok
> And at myn herte.   [BD 837–41

She is a lady without physical or moral blemish, true and sincere, the friend of virtuous behaviour; neither solemn nor skittish, but respecting moderation in all things. Although her beauty gives her a ready power over men, she refuses to compromise with truth and honesty by acting the coquette with her suitors. Love and respect impel the young knight to dedicate himself to the lady's service, though as yet he does not attempt to make his passion known to her. Instead, he strains every nerve

> To love hir in my beste wyse,
> To do hir worship and the servise
> That I koude thoo, be my trouthe,
> Withoute feynynge outher slouthe.
>   [BD 1097–100

Throughout this period of dutiful service the lady remains ignorant of her lover's feelings, since he dare not disclose himself to her, and can only express himself through the songs which he composes to give relief to his undeclared love. Eventually, encouraged by the idea that Nature never gives beauty without kindness, he confesses his passion to the lady in fear and misgiving:

> Softe and quakynge for pure drede
> And shame, and styntynge in my tale
> For ferde, and myn hewe al pale.
>   [BD 1212–14

But the attempt is unsuccessful: the lady refuses him, and for a long while he lives in constant misery. After a year of suffering

he decides to make another attempt to win her, and on this
occasion he is able to convince her of his selfless desire to serve
and honour her:

> That I ne wilned thyng but god,
> And worship, and to kepe hir name
> Over alle thyng, and drede hir shame,
> And was so besy hyr to serve.
>
> [BD 1262–5

At this the lady accepts him as her lover; and he finds complete
happiness in the deep understanding and harmony of their
relationship, which unites them in mutual joy for many years
before the worst kind of misfortune strikes at the lover. When
the puzzled dreamer persists in asking for a plain explanation
of the personal disaster which has driven the Man in Black into
the solitude of the forest, he learns what the reader has known
from the beginning. The lady is dead. As this surprise is sprung
at him, the dreamer is jerked into recollection of the hunt
which brought him into the forest, and a final horn-blast recalls
him to the crowd of courtly riders and attendants who are now
withdrawing from the woods:

> And with that word ryght anoon
> They gan to strake forth; al was doon,
> For that tyme, the hert-huntyng.
>
> [BD 1311–13

The Man in Black disappears from his dream, and the dreamer
is reabsorbed into the calvalcade as it returns to the 'long castel'
by which Chaucer alludes cryptically to Lancaster and the
ostensible occasion of his poem. As they approach the castle a
bell strikes twelve and the dreamer awakes, to find himself in
bed and still holding the book over which he had fallen asleep:
a conclusion which brings the poem back to the *Paradys d'Amours*
which also provides its starting-point.

From the dreamer's meeting with the Man in Black to this
final point of the poem Chaucer's dependence upon Machaut is
almost continuous, both generally and in numerous details of
courtly outlook and comment. A lament by a bereaved or

rejected lover figures conspicuously in several of Machaut's poems,[1] and both the *Remede de Fortune* and the *Roy de Behaingne* contain detailed descriptions of the lady's character and appearance. Chaucer does not attempt to parallel these descriptions in his own terms, but follows Machaut almost as a translator. The Man in Black's account of his first sight of the lady, 'I sawgh hyr daunce so comlily', repeats Machaut almost word for word:

> Car je la vi dancier cointement
> Et puis chanter si trés joliement,
> Rire et jouer si gracieusement,
> Qu'onques encor
> Ne fu veu plus gracieus tresor. [RB 297–301

By combining features of two of Machaut's poems Chaucer builds up a picture of the lady, and of the lover's agonised hopes, in close conformity with a courtly ideal of feminine beauty and of the humble adoration which the lady should inspire in her lover; but without apparently expressing any idea of his own. There is some originality in Chaucer's situation, for Machaut does not present the lover's complaint in the context of a dream; and in his story the cause of the lover's grief is too self-evident for the narrative to end in a surprising disclosure. In *The Boke of the Duchesse* the surprise is made possible by the dreamer's obtuseness and unfamiliarity with the conventions of *fine amour*, qualities in which Machaut shows no interest. The bereaved lady of the *Roy de Behaingne* tells her story to a king, who judges between her unhappy experience and that of a knight betrayed and abandoned by his mistress; and in the *Dit de la Fonteinne Amoureuse* another distracted lover, later identified as a duke, is supported and encouraged by the arguments of a courteous and understanding friend. The novelty of Chaucer's version of the *comfort d'ami* lies in the disparity of his two characters, and in the fact that the dreamer's incomprehension makes

---

[1] Most prominently in the *Fonteinne Amoureuse*, the *Remede de Fortune*, the *Dit dou Lyon* and the *Roy de Behaingne*.

him unable to provide the comfort which he offers. His comments on the knight's story demonstrate how far he is out of touch with the tradition of behaviour so respectfully observed by this mourning lover, and how inadequately he responds to a situation made familiar by several French poets.

The dreamer's undiplomatic manner is well displayed by his brief interruption of the story in lines 1042–51. The knight has been explaining how completely he was committed to the lady, 'that swete wif', finding in her the embodiment of all worldly happiness:

> My suffisaunce, my lust, my lyf,
> Myn hap, myn hele, and al my blesse,
> My worldes welfare, and my goddesse.
>
> [BD 1038–40

The dreamer tries to indicate his appreciation of this unreserved worship, but the impulse of such absolute devotion is clearly beyond him, and his comment merely creates an impression of well-meaning heartiness. 'By oure lord,' he exclaims approvingly,

> 'y trowe yow wel!
> Hardely, your love was wel beset:
> I not how ye myghte have do bet.'   [BD 1042–4

The knight does not allow this under-statement to pass uncorrected. 'Bet?' he repeats as though indignantly, 'ne no wyght so wel!' and the dreamer quickly adopts the correction, apologising for his slip. Under pressure from the knight's insistently idealistic references to the lady, the dreamer then makes a valiant effort to express his sympathy with the attitudes of *fine amour*; but his comment only succeeds in putting the knight's extremism in perspective. 'I leve yow wel,' he agrees,

> 'that trewely
> Yow thoghte that she was the beste,
> And to beholde the alderfayreste,
> Whoso had loked hir with your eyen.'
>
> [BD 1048–51

The knight protests at the moderation of the remark, but resumes his story; until some fifty lines later another ill-judged observation throws him out of his stride. He has been telling how a glimpse of his lady early in the day could keep him happy until the night, and put all troubles out of mind. Evidently the dreamer feels that a comment is expected of him, and he rises to the occasion with a clumsily and half-jocular compliment that is badly out of keeping with the dedicated spirit of the tale:

> 'Now, by my trouthe, sir!' quod I,
> 'Me thynketh ye have such a chaunce
> As shryfte wythoute repentaunce.'   [BD 1112–4

He means, presumably, that the knight has enjoyed the inward happiness of a man newly confessed but without the anguish of repentance; but the parallel has unfortunate associations which the Man in Black takes up at once, sensing a slur on his constancy as a lover. 'Repentaunce? nay, fie!' he exclaims,

> 'Shulde y now repente me
> To love? Nay, certes, than were I wel
> Wers than was Achitofel,
> Or Anthenor, so have I joye,
> The traytor that betraysed Troye.'   [BD 1116–20

The far-fetched comparisons and the tone of the knight's rebuke show how badly the dreamer has misjudged the situation, and how foreign the outlook of courtly love is to his way of thinking. This disparity of outlook declares itself most openly during the first and most extensive of the dreamer's interruptions, when he breaks out in protest against the knight's self-abandoning grief, imploring him to feel some concern for his physical well-being:

> 'Have som pitee on your nature
> That formed yow to creature!'   [BD 715–16

His protest picks up an idea heard several times previously, beginning with an early remark of the speaker's that to live in his state of sleepless depression is 'agaynes kynde'. The theme is touched on again when he meets the Man in Black, and feels

astonished that nature could allow one of its creatures to continue living under the strain of such grief. This comment might
be meant to arouse respect for the utterly despondent lover; but
when the dreamer continues by describing the physiological
cause of the knight's swooning he seems rather to suggest
nature's hostility to a code of behaviour which encourages such
profound self-neglect:

> The blood was fled for pure drede
> Doun to hys herte, to make hym warm –
> For wel hyt feled the herte had harm –
> To wite eke why hyt was adrad
> By kynde, and for to make hyt glad.   [BD 490–4

Like the dreamer in his attempts to revive the knight's almost
extinguished concern for his own existence, the blood is trying
to warm and comfort the knight's heart, and so repulse the
melancholy which seems likely to destroy him. The phrase 'by
kynde' underlines the natural anxiety felt by the body for its
'membre principal', almost overwhelmed by unresisted despair;
and tacitly invites us to recognise the unnaturalness of the code
which the Man in Black is observing so faithfully. The point is
made again a little later, when the dreamer, explaining that the
knight was almost out of his mind with grief, adds:

> Thogh Pan, that men clepe god of kynde,
> Were for his sorwes never so wroth.   [BD 512–13

As god of 'kynde' or natural impulse, Pan has reason to be
angry with a form of suicidal depression which attacks the
victim's will to live. When the dreamer makes his own protest
against such lack of self-regard, he develops the objection with
a good deal of energy. 'Thogh ye had lost the ferses twelve,' he
argues, evidently confused by the knight's reference to chess.

> 'And ye for sorwe mordered yourselve,
> Ye sholde be dampned in this cas
> By as good ryght as Medea was,
> That slough hir children for Jasoun;
> And Phyllis also for Demophoun

Heng hirself, so weylaway!
For he had broke his terme-day
To come to hir. Another rage
Had Dydo, the quene eke of Cartage,
That slough hirself, for Eneas
Was fals: which a fool she was!
And Ecquo died, for Narcisus
Nolde nat love hir; and ryght thus
Hath many another foly doon.'   [BD 724-37

This scornfully depreciative judgement of romantic suicide
shows more clearly than any other of the dreamer's remarks
how fundamentally he is opposed to the standards of *fine amour*.
The passage represents a head-on collision with the tradition
which the Man in Black adopts unquestioningly, accepting the
risk of death to pay his dead mistress the tribute of unrestrained
grief. Against this self-sacrificing idealism the dream raises his
own standard of commonsense and moderation, dismissing the
concept of noble death by sorrow as sheer nonsense: 'Which
a fool she was!' He has forgotten that in his waking experience
he found the death of Alcyone supremely touching. This con-
temptuous phrase must make it very difficult to argue that the
dreamer realises what lies behind the knight's inconsolable
sadness: if he does, he is behaving sadistically. It is much easier
to believe that in his general ignorance of *fine amour* the dreamer
does not realise that the knight shares the outlook of the lovers
whose respect for constancy the dreamer derides. When he warns
the knight against the danger of being damned as a suicide, the
dreamer proves himself unaware that the knight would be
much more deeply dishonoured by a failure to mourn his lady
to the point of death.

In allowing the dreamer to make this attack on a central
principle of courtly love, Chaucer had some encouragement
from Machaut. In the *Roy de Behaingne* the rightness of the
bereaved lady's grief is not questioned: the point at issue is
whether her plight is more painful than that of the lover whose
mistress has betrayed him. But in the *Jugement dou Roy de
Navarre*, which challenges the decision reached in the previous

poem, Machaut himself argues that natural law gives a bereaved
lover the right to put his sorrow behind him, since no extremity
of grief can restore what he has lost:

> Et si say moult bien que Nature
> A de son bon droit establi
> Qu'on mettre celui en oubli
> Qui est mors et n'en puet ravoir
> Pour grant peinne, ne pour avoir.   [RN 2070–4

The next speaker in the debate resists this opinion, but first
defends the judgement that no distress or pain is comparable to
that of a lady deserted by her faithless lover. To support her
argument, Pais cites the example of Dido, 'roine de Cartage',
who

> Ot si grant dueil et si grant rage
> Pour l'amour qu'elle ot a Enée
> Qui li avoit sa foy donée
> Qu'a mouillier l'aroit et a femme.
>
> [RN 2096–9

The phrase 'si grant rage' seems to have found its way into the
corresponding passage of *The Boke of the Duchesse*, together with
Machaut's collective reference to other victims of faithless lovers
who took their own lives in grief and desperation:

> Einsi com pluseurs amans font
> Qui l'amant loial contrefont,
> La desesperée, la fole,
> Qu'amours honnist, qu'amours afole.
>
> [RN 2109–12

The speaker is expressing sympathy with Dido in the cruel
treatment which drove her to suicide, and not – like Chaucer's
dreamer – declaring such behaviour absurd. But the passage in
the *Roy de Navarre* could be made to serve that purpose, and
associated with the argument put forward by Machaut in his
own person, approving the good sense of lovers who put a term
to their grief:

> Et mort d'amant et mort d'amie
> Pour ce qu'on n'i puet recouvrer
> Par grant avoir, ne par ouvrer.   [RN 2168–70

The same realistic attitude is expressed by the ghost of Seys in Chaucer's version of the myth, when he advises Alcyone to make an end of lamentations which can benefit no one. When Machaut re-tells the same story in his *Fonteinne Amoreuse*, however, we hear nothing of this practical attitude, for he presents a Ceyx who invokes pity for his miserable fate, and even forbids Alcyone to reflect upon the uselessness of complaining:

> 'Resgarde moy, et de moy te souveingne.
> Ne pense pas, bele, qu'en vain me plaigne:
> Voy mes cheveus, voy ma barbe grifaingne;
>   Voy mon habit
> Que de ma mort te moustre vraie enseigne!'
> [FA 675–9

Comparison reveals how Chaucer has developed the dreamer's point of view. The good sense of Seys' advice to his heartbroken wife in *The Boke of the Duchesse* has the backing of Machaut's contention in the *Roy de Navarre* that natural law commands the grieving lover to take thought for his own survival by forgetting his sorrow. The dreamer of Chaucer's poem repeats this argument, which he has previously found in the spectral husband's speech to Alcyone, when he urges the Man in Black to 'have som pitee' for himself, and attacks the folly of those who abandon themselves to despair. But this attack on romantic tradition goes a good deal further than Machaut's criticism, and is expressed in terms much less courtly than the French speaker employs. By his roughness of speech, as by his failure to grasp the significance of the knight's misery, the dreamer makes himself appear a comic intruder upon a situation too delicate for his commonplace apparatus of feeling; but by this means Chaucer establishes the polarity that is central to his purposes.

This polarity involves the states of sleeping and waking in the contradictory relationship that has already been noted. At the beginning of the poem the dreamer is physically awake, but

so confused and self-absorbed that he seems cut off from solid
reality as though in fact dreaming. When he eventually falls
asleep his fogged awareness is suddenly replaced by a sharp
clarity of outlook and an excited impulse to throw himself into
a vigorous activity more representative of waking life than of
dreaming. These two opposing states of being are associated
with equally conflicting states of mind. The initial dreamlike
dazedness comes from an inability to sleep, which is in turn
produced by a profound depression: 'sorwful ymagynacioun',
so disabling that the dreamer senses a threat to his life. The
story of Alcyone describes another victim of the same malaise.
Almost out of her mind with distress, 'forweped and forwaked'
in her fear that Seys may be dead, the queen puts her life in
hazard by continuous lamentation. When the spectral Seys tries
to remind her of her obligations to life, his peremptory 'Awake!'
implies that Alcyone is morally asleep, and self-blinded to the
primary law of nature which binds all creatures. The Man in
Black shares her perverse determination to refuse all comfort or
hope of cure. 'Ne hele me may no phisicien,' he tells the
dreamer, 'noght Ypocras, ne Galyen,'

> 'My lyf, my lustes, be me loothe,
> For al welfare and I be wroothe.'   [BD 581–2

This deliberate rejection of medicine and healthy remedies
justifies the dreamers' warning that if the knight kills himself
through self-neglect he may be damned; for although he mis-
interprets the situation, the dreamer recognises the natural law
that is outraged when grief is allowed to dominate over the
positive impulses of life. The Man in Black too is morally
asleep, as he suggests by failing to notice the dreamer or to
acknowledge his greeting; immobilised by depression as by a
drug which destroys the desire to remain alive. The polarity is
completed by the association of waking with enthusiastic parti-
cipation in active affairs, and with acceptance of natural law as
opposed to the artificial code of manners which directs *fine
amour*. The self-destructive melancholy which the lover induces
in himself makes him unaware of his folly in frustrating the

purposes of natural life. He needs to waken into awareness of his moral obligation to respect life more than death, and to commit himself to the goings-on about him, as Chaucer's dreamer does when he wakes into the bustle of preparations for a royal hunt.

From this it appears that the narrator of *The Boke of the Duchesse* is most truly a dreamer before he falls asleep over his book, and that in his actual dream his physical energy and his respect for 'kynde' associate him strongly with wide-awake consciousness. When he wakes into the warmth and brilliance of a summer morning, and responds to the exhilarating challenge of the hunting-horn, he breaks away from the despondency and inertia which had previously given his life the unreality of a dream. The man whom he finds in the depths of the forest, motionless and withdrawn, has yielded himself to stagnation like the derelicts in Morpheus' cave, who sleep and do 'noon other werk', and who cannot release themselves from their self-willed paralysis. As a dream-poem, *The Boke of the Duchesse* is thus something of a paradox. Although 'a wonder thyng', describing an unearthly vision of noble constancy in love, the poem associates dreaming with a state of moral obliviousness and physical inertia which frustrates the purposes of natural life, and urges respect for the creative impulse which renews all living things after the ordeal of winter. Immediately before his meeting with the Man in Black, the dreamer comments on the surge of vitality which has covered the earth with fresh flowers:

> Hyt had forgete the povertee
> That wynter, thorgh hys colde morwes,
> Had mad hyt suffre, and his sorwes;
> All was forgeten, and that was sene:
> For al the wode was waxen grene.   [BD 410–14

The dreamer's observations, to be used again in *The Legend of Good Women*,[1] are a poetic commonplace deriving from the *Roman de la Rose*, but the borrowed passage plays its part in the

[1] *LGW* F.125–9

tacit argument of *The Boke of the Duchesse*. It is clear that
Chaucer's poem presents an implicit criticism of the standards
of *fine amour* as well as some encouragement to feel compassion
for the Man in Black in his bleak desolation of spirit. Both the
seasonal cycle and the law of kind to which the dreamer appeals
recognise a need to forget sorrow in the greater interest of continuing life: a need which conflicts with an indispensable condition of *fine amour*, as the dreamer gradually discovers. When
Machaut argues against the ideal of suicidal constancy in the
Roy de Navarre he is perhaps trailing his coat, or acting as a
devil's advocate; but whatever his purpose he is speaking inside
the circle of courtly society whose code is being debated. In
Chaucer's poem the code is being resisted by a figure who, if not
an outsider, has a very imperfect knowledge of courtly conventions, and who shares the practical outlook voiced by the
ghost of Seys in telling Alcyone that her grief serves no useful
end. This commonsense advice is added unobtrusively to the
speech which Chaucer took from Ovid or from Machaut's
version of the myth: the first indication of the critical pressure
which Chaucer brings to bear upon a tradition of noble behaviour and romantic love.

At the same time it indicates, at Chaucer's setting-out as a
poet, the tension between courtly ideals and the demands of
everyday life from which springs much of the comic energy of
his later work. The code is not rejected; and the fact that *The
Boke of the Duchesse* has for so long been read as a straightforward
tribute to John of Gaunt in his bereavement proves how successfully Chaucer has obscured his equivocal attitude towards the
emotional extremism which dominates the Man in Black's
story. The figure who expresses the explicit criticism of the
lover's extravagant grief seems a half-comic intruder upon a
world whose sensitive feelings he only dimly discerns. His
manner encourages us to regard him as something of an
irrelevance, at best as a device to elicit the story which takes up
most of the poem; but here, as in *The Hous of Fame* and *The
Parlement of Foules*, the dreamer's unimpressive individuality,
and his apparently subordinate role in the dream itself, give a

misleading idea of his importance. By representing the values
and outlook of a more prosaic reality, he throws into relief the
romantic ideals of the dream-world to which he is briefly
admitted; and brings courtly tradition into contact with the
incongruous figures and attitudes of practical affairs, where the
dream is tested against waking truth.

How is the dream tested against waking truth.?
what do you mean?
Dreamer's experience is divided against the world's of fact; fancy C- shape of a dream.

III

THE HOUS OF FAME

THE opening of Chaucer's second dream-poem is full of surprises. Putting aside the gravity appropriate to a vision, the
narrator of *The Hous of Fame* assumes completely the comic
persona occasionally seen in *The Boke of the Duchesse*, and begins
the poem with a long profession of ignorance which disproves
itself. The cause and significance of dreams, the speaker declares,
what distinguishes a 'fantome' from an oracular vision, and
what learned opinions have been offered on this complex subject, are all beyond him; but the length of this disclaimer, and
the familiarity with technical terms and scholarly argument
which it displays, show Chaucer indulging in a characteristic
joke. Remembering the dreamer's pretended ignorance about
Juno's husband in *The Boke of the Duchesse*, we recognise the
same comic attitude here, greatly extended and given a pro-
minent place as the opening fifty lines of a more ambitious
poem. Chaucer might be serving notice from the outset that
The Hous of Fame is to be dominated by a comic purpose, and
announcing a decision to break away from the courtly tradition
of the dream-poem, which even in the previous work is under
strain. Neither of these seeming promises is entirely fulfilled;
but the elaborate parade of ignorance which opens the poem,
with its mock deference to the 'grete clerkys' whose opinions
might be sought, represents the mode through which Chaucer's
comic genius is to find typical expression.

The second surprise lies in the sudden transition from waking
to sleeping. 'Of Decembre the tenthe day', the dreamer begins
his story, dating his adventure with the exactness which
Chaucer had found in Machaut,[1]

---

[1] Compare *Dit dou Lyon* 32: 'Dou mois d'avril le jour secont'; *Roy de*

Whan hit was nyght, to slepe I lay
Ryght ther as I was wont to done,
And fil on slepe wonder sone. [HF 112–14

After the example of *The Boke of the Duchesse*, with nearly three
hundred lines of preliminaries to the dream, this immediate
onset of sleep seems abrupt and even impatient. Although the
narrator is not troubled by insomnia as in the previous poem,
we might expect Chaucer to exploit the relationship between
the dreamer's preoccupations asleep and awake, as he does
there, making those conscious interests influence or determine
the form of the subsequent dream. The absence of such waking
interests appears more surprising by comparison with *The Parlement of Foules*, where the dream is again preceded by an account
of the narrator's activities during the day, and a summary of
his reading. There as in *The Boke of the Duchesse* the dreamer's
experience is divided between the worlds of fact and fantasy,
whose apparently unrelated figures and happenings are linked
through the book which shapes the initial form of the dream.
Chaucer's reasons for giving waking life no place in *The Hous of
Fame* are not easily suggested. Lacking any reference to the
dreamer's waking interests, we must look for an explanation of
his curious adventure within the dream itself.

Book I purports to be a description of the marvellous Temple
of Venus in which the dreamer finds himself on falling asleep.
In fact the account of the mural decoration of the temple is
much more like an erratic summary of the opening books of the
Aeneid, with a realistic commentary by the dreamer which
implies a much closer acquaintance with common life than he
is allowed later in the poem. To the extent that the great mural
painting treats the theme of romantic love in the story of Dido's
passion for Aeneas, the dream merges with the traditional love-
vision; but this topic is not sustained in either of the two books
which follow. Book II describes the dreamer's eye-opening flight
across the heavens in the Eagle's claws to the Hous of Fame, the
gathering-point of all the noises and speeches uttered on earth.

Navarre 25: 'Le novisme jour de novembre'. Unlike Chaucer, Machaut
also gives the year.

It includes a verbatim report of the Eagle's lecture on the nature of sound, which occupies most of the journey: a typically Chaucerian display of learning, offered in a jocular spirit to a dreamer now thoroughly awed by his alarming adventure and by the huge though affable creature which has taken charge of him. Book III comprises three separate episodes. It begins with more architectural wonders as the dreamer reaches Fame's House, and then lists the statues of famous writers and chroniclers which he finds inside – in some respects a repetition of his commentary in Book I. It continues with a lively description of Fame's judgement of her suitors, which shows the dreamer how arbitrarily the goddess awards her favours. The original concern with romantic love, and Venus with her 'rose garlond whit and red', is now entirely forgotten; and the topic remains inert in the final episode of Book III, which brings the dreamer to the whirling House of Rumour and its ceaselessly chattering occupants. At this point the narrative breaks off, leaving the poem and the dream together unfinished.

The different episodes of the poem are so dissimilar in content that a first reading of *The Hous of Fame* may suggest a lack of unifying purpose. This impression is strengthened by the uncertainty of the dreamer's character, which fluctuates so much over the course of the three books that different narrators might be involved. As the beginning of his adventure the dreamer expresses the typical puzzlement of a man suddenly deprived of familiar surroundings, though able to recognise the goddess who is the principal inspiration of poetry:

> For certeynly, I nyste never
> Wher that I was, but wel wyste I
> Hyt was of Venus redely
> The temple; for in portreyture
> I sawgh anoon-ryght hir figure
> Naked fleytynge in a see.   [HF 128–33

This admission of confusion about his whereabouts is repeated at the end of Book I, when the dreamer leaves the temple unable to imagine who could have created the astonishing work of art

covering its walls. But although he professes such surprise and
incomprehension –

> 'A, Lord!' thoughte I, 'that madest us,
> Yet sawgh I never such noblesse
> Of ymages, ne such richesse,
> As I saugh graven in this chirche!'   [HF 470–3

– his description of the Virgilian mural suggests a long-standing
acquaintance with the story which it depicts; and the dreamer
is clearly more interested in retelling the tale of Dido and
Aeneas than in describing any 'richesse' of painted scenes.[1]
Throughout much of Book I the dreamer who declares himself
mystified by the beauty and master-craftsmanship of the temple
is at variance with a second aspect of himself as bookish scholar,
well acquainted with 'Virgile in Eneydos', whose reading could
evidently have supplied the missing prelude to his dream. The
Virgilian mural is both the wonderful matter of the dreamer's
vision and the familiar reading of his waking-life self, who relates
the tale with no obvious enthusiasm for romantic passion. There
are other indications that the dreamer is in wide-awake contact
with actuality while he is describing the temple. The story of
Dido is not presented to him as part of an astonishing vision,
with himself as dumbfounded spectator. When the charm of
pictorial description wears thin, he takes charge of the narrative
himself and finishes the tale in his own realistic terms; showing
no inclination to exploit the pathos of Dido's situation despite
his professed excitement. When it comes to the point, the
'figures of olde werk' which he marvels at are rapidly disposed
of, and replaced by a critically detached summary of Dido's

---

[1] The probable source of Chaucer's mural painting is suggested in a
more respectful version of Dido's story, in LGW 1023–6: 'And whan this
Eneas and Achates/Hadden in this temple ben overal,/Thanne founden
they, depeynted on a wal,/How Troye and al the lond destroyed was.'
This follows *Aeneid* I. 457 ff., a passage whose account of Juno's temple
with its bronze doors and rich craftsmanship may have contributed to
Chaucer's picture of the Temple of Venus. The Virgilian Aeneas, who
'viewed with wonder all those scenes, rooted in a deep trance of attention',
is suggestively akin to this dreamer in his response to another version of
the same painted scenes.

story which has few dreamlike qualities. Although nominally
asleep, he retains enough awareness of the world of fact to advise
his readers where to find a fuller version of Dido's speech before
her death; and then ignores his fictional situation even more
completely by regretting that the speech is too long to be
quoted in his own poem:

> And nere hyt to long to endyte,
> Be God, I wolde hyt here write.   [HF 381–2

Instead, he contents himself with a worldly-wise comment on
the distress caused by inconstancy in love; a subject frequently
treated in books, and an everyday occurrence in the world at
large:

> But wel-away! the harm, the routhe,
> That hath betyd for such untrouthe,
> As men may ofte in bokes rede,
> And al day sen hyt yet in dede.   [HF 383–6

With this observant eye on the common happenings of life, and
on the necessary limits of his poem, the narrator can hardly be
asleep and much less dreaming. The tale of Dido evokes none
of the characteristic wonder of a dream, nor even the waking
astonishment which the story of Alcyone arouses in the narrator of *The Boke of the Duchesse*. Instead, it prompts the dreamer
to offer a general commentary on the unwisdom of crediting a
stranger's profession of love, followed by a catalogue of examples matching Dido's shameful mistreatment. These digres-
sions from the description of the temple weaken the dreamer's
story still further, both by distracting attention from the dream
and by proving his familiarity with the practical realities of life.
It is no bewildered visionary who makes this experienced
appraisal of man's treachery, but a speaker whose worldliness
and vocabulary foreshadow Chaucer's final embodiment of
commonsense judgement:

> Loo, how a womman doth amys
> To love him that unknowen ys!
> For, be Cryste, lo, thus yt fareth:

'Hyt is not al gold that glareth.'
For also browke I wel myn hed,
Ther may be under godlyhed
Kevered many a shrewed vice.   [HF 269–75

However relevant to everyday affairs, these snatches of proverbial wisdom have no bearing upon the world of fantasy
through which the dreamer has been moving. They represent
the terms of prosaic reality, not of dreams; and in assuming a
didactic attitude the speaker implies a well-tried familiarity
with his subject, and not a dreamer's bewilderment. He shows
the same certainty of judgement in his catalogue of cases
parallel to Dido's:

How fals eke was he Theseus,
That, as the story telleth us,
How he betrayed Adriane;
The devel be hys soules bane!   [HF 405–8

This explosive comment associates the speaker with the market-
place, not with the ethereal world of a love-vision, and its
shifted interest reveals how far the dreamer has wandered
from his description of the Virgilian frescoes. The dream which
began in awed wonder has now descended to an indignant
review of man's sexual opportunism, with illustrations taken
from famous love-stories. In this respect Book I combines the
same incompatible attitudes as *The Boke of the Duchesse* in its
confrontation of dreamer and knight. The glass temple and its
vast mural painting, comprising innumerable individual figures
and scenes, belong to a literary tradition running strongly from
the most influential of love-visions. The dreamer's worldly
experience and realistic judgement are alien to this tradition;
and where in his previous dream-poem Chaucer embodies these
conflicting points of view in two different characters, in the
opening section of *The Hous of Fame* the same figure is both
dreamer and spokesman for reality.

By the end of his summary the narrator hardly bothers to
maintain his pretence of describing painted scenes, and concludes the story of Aeneas by remarking that

F

The book seyth Mercurie, sauns fayle,
Bad hym goo into Itayle;

[HF 429-30

presenting the tale in the terms most natural to him. This
explicit reference to 'the book' and the passages of direct speech
given to Dido, indicate plainly enough where Chaucer's personal interests lie. If Book I has any dominant purpose, it could
be an impulse to re-tell the story of Dido, as though in honour
of the goddess whose picture, 'naked fletynge in a see', identifies
her temple. But the dreamer's account of Dido's behaviour
cannot be reconciled with the traditions of the love-vision
which the opening of the dream suggests. As an epic theme
dwindles into a garbled tale of incautious love betrayed, a
legendary figure of romance declines to the prosaic level at
which she can moralise upon the foolish susceptibility of all
women to false oaths. 'Now see I wel, and telle kan,' she declares
after her betrayal by Aeneas,

> 'We wrechched wymmen konne noon art;
> For certeyn, for the more part,
> Thus we be served everychone.'   [HF 335-7

This homely comment does not characterise the idiom of romantic grief and suicide. Here as in *The Boke of the Duchesse*, Chaucer's
dreamer shows himself incapable of grasping the nobility of
Dido's response to private disaster, and fails entirely to appre-
ciate the unworldly ideals of courtly love. The heroine of this
mundane story laments not because her lover has proved in-
constant, but because she must be remembered as a woman
dishonoured by an imprudent liaison with a stranger. 'O wel-
awey that I was born!' she cries, rebuking the faithless Aeneas,

> 'For thorgh yow is my name lorn,
> And alle myn actes red and songe
> Over al thys lond, on every tonge.
> O wikke Fame! for ther nys
> Nothing so swift, lo, as she is!
> O, soth ys, every thing ys wyst,
> Though hit be kevered with the myst.

Eke, though I myghte duren ever,
That I have don, rekever I never,
That I ne shal be seyd, allas,
Yshamed be thourgh Eneas.'

[HF 346–356

Dido's fears are mistaken. Although the tragic tale of her love is
to be read and sung throughout time, except in obtusely critical
versions of the story such as the dreamer offers here, Dido's
reputation will not suffer. To the contrary, as Chaucer was well
aware, poets from Virgil onwards would assure that she was
remembered with sympathy and respect, as a woman whose
death proved both her fidelity to Aeneas and her heartbroken
grief at being deserted. Within the traditions of courtly romance
no reputation could be more secure. But evidently it suited
Chaucer's purposes to twist the legend into a new shape, ignoring both the actual nature of Dido's reputation and its very
considerable dependence upon the poets who repeated her
story, and suggesting that 'wikke Fame' would see that only a
shameful memory of her name persisted.

Chaucer's interest in fame is admitted in the title of his poem,
though this does not suggest the complexity of the term. In
Middle English, beside referring to reputation and renown,
'fame' had the now obsolete sense of 'noise'; and in the celestial
Hous to which the dreamer is transported the two qualities are
closely associated. Since medieval poetry was commonly spoken
rather than read silently, noise may have an implicit connection
with the poet's work. This likelihood seems to be confirmed
when, after learning from the Eagle that 'tidings' of human
affairs are indispensable to the poet, the dreamer discovers that
the source of universal tidings which he has been brought to
hear in the House of Rumour is a deafening noise. It appears
that the 'Fame' of Chaucer's title is the starting-point of a chain
of associated ideas running through all three parts of the poem,
and that Dido's attack on the agency which will broadcast her
disgrace provides a link between Book I and the rest of the
dreamer's adventure. The link is not substantial: but it might
be easier to account for Chaucer's unconventional treatment of

Dido if an imaginative concern with 'fame' in all its senses were directing the course of the poem. Even without this clarification of his purposes, it becomes possible to recognise the shape of Chaucer's interests when the dreamer ends his survey of the temple by confessing his ignorance of the master-craftsman responsible for the 'noblesse of ymages' which he has been studying:

> But not wot I whoo did hem wirche.   [HF 474

We might object that his own allusion to 'Virgile in Eneydos' establishes the authorship of the figures plainly enough, but evidently the speaker has reverted to his original persona and knows nothing much about anything. In itself, his remark collides ironically with Dido's dread of future fame, and with the inscription cut 'on a table of bras' inside the temple, announcing the poet's intention to relate the story of Aeneas. While he and Dido are remembered, the artist's name is lost and commemorated only by his marvellous but anonymous work. Moved by curiosity and a desire to know where he is, the dreamer decides to leave the temple 'ryght at the wiket' in the hope of finding a passer-by to enlighten him; but outside a shock awaits him:

> Then sawgh I but a large feld
> As fer as that I myghte see,
> Withouten toun, or hous, or tree,
> Or bush, or gras, or eryd lond . . .
> Ne no maner creature
> That ys yformed be Nature
> Ne sawgh I, me to rede or wisse.   [HF 482–91

From the plenitude of art about which he has just made a delighted comment, the dreamer passes to a sterile expanse of sandy desert, empty of life, and offering him no hope of enlightenment. The vacancy confronting him reflects the ignorance which he admits at the beginning of his dream and which the Eagle is to rebuke: a state which seems to have been deepened by his study of the frescoes. Once he leaves the visionary world of the unknown artist, with its inexhaustible richness of figures and events, the dreamer becomes suddenly and disconcertingly aware of the limitations of his private experience, and the paucity of his creative power. Unnerved by the emptiness which faces him, he offers a prayer to be rescued from the futility of his private situation:

> 'O Crist!' thoughte I, 'that art in blysse,
> Fro fantome and illusion
> Me save!' and with devocion
> Myn eyen to the hevene I caste.   [HF 492–5

If Chaucer is using 'fantome' in the same sense here and at the beginning of Book I, the dreamer is in the paradoxical position of asking to be rescued from a meaningless *phantasma*, which has abruptly replaced his love-vision in the temple. But the love-vision has been an equivocal experience, constantly shifting from 'portreytures' to narrative; and the dreamer is now in the situation of a reader who has finished an astonishing work of poetry in the galling realisation that his own writing is trivial and untalented. This significance of his appeal to be delivered from 'fantome and illusion' appears when, in direct answer, he is given the instructive experience which he needs as a poet. Contact with a great work of literature has disclosed craftsmanship of an order hitherto beyond the dreamer's scope, and he is anxious not to remain imprisoned in the featureless world of a minor talent. The Eagle obligingly rescues him from this uncreative desert.

Up to this point Chaucer has not suggested that his dreamer is a practising poet, but from here on his literary aspirations become a matter of some comic importance. The first indication of this new element in the dreamer's character is seen in the Proem to Book II, whose special interest has already been considered. In respect to the narrative it stands in a curious position athwart the story-line, and interrupting the development on which Book I unexpectedly closes. Looking upwards at the end of his prayer,

> as hye
> As kenne myghte I with myn ye,   [HF 497–8

and half-blinded by the sun, the dreamer discerns the form of a great eagle; and in the final line of the passage he sees the bird beginning to descend, as though in response to his appeal. It is still at a great distance, and moving without haste when the narrator breaks off his story and addresses his audience, promising to describe 'so sely an avisyon' as no previous dreamer, whether

> Isaye, ne Scipion,
> Ne kyng Nabugodonosor,
> Pharoo, Turnus, ne Elcanor,   [HF 514–16

had encountered. This preface is appreciably more excited than the modest claim which introduces the previous section of the poem, and the emphasis of the assertion suggests that the poet has only now reached the point where his dream begins. As though to nerve himself for the task of relating so wonderful a vision, he invokes the support of Venus, the Muses, and finally of the human faculty which 'wrot' or created his dream; a force which must now prove itself a second time by giving form and expression to an incredible experience:

> now shal men se
> Yf any vertu in the be
> To tellen al my drem aryght.
> Now kythe thyn engyn and myght!   [HF 525–8

The challenge is answered as promptly as his prayer for divine assistance, which it duplicates in different terms; and by the same vigorous means. As the dreamer returns to his story, the great bird drops on him like a thunderbolt, grabs him as though he were as inconsequential as an eggshell, and soars back into the sky without checking his flight. The transformation of the Eagle from a remote and mainly decorative figure into the irresistible force which seizes the dreamer in the opening lines of Book II calls for some comment. When the dreamer first sees him, the Eagle is idling in the heavens high above him, and only the closing line of Book I, 'And somwhat dounward gan hyt lyghte', indicates that the bird may be moving towards him.

When the story is resumed after the Proem, the Eagle is rushing towards the dreamer with the speed of a cannon-ball, and about to snatch him up in mid-flight 'as lightly as I were a larke'. The imaginative effect of his sequence, extending over lines 495–546, is to suggest that the headlong descent of the bird has been impelled not just by the dreamer's prayer but by the parallel appeal to his 'Thought', which has been answered by this unmistakable demonstration of 'engyn and myght'. This suggestion is strengthened by what follows, as the Eagle explains that his purpose is to reward the dreamer's persistent efforts to show reverence for Love by composing 'bookys, songes, dytees' in his honour; which he will do by supplying the missing experience which his poetry needs. This promised 'recompensacion' for the dreamer's well-meant efforts in the past, which begins when the Eagle rescues the dreamer from sterile vacancy and ends with the dreamer surrounded by a shouting multitude, is brought into existence by the poet's 'Thought' or creative imagination as it rises to the special challenge voiced in the Proem. The dominant part played by the Eagle in the same process leaves no doubt about his symbolic function.

As the dreamer is borne aloft by the splendid creature which has taken control of him, he acquires a more definite personality than either of his counterparts in the two other Chaucerian dream-poems. Instead of remaining an anonymous observer required to register interest and astonishment on the poet's behalf, he becomes himself a subject observed and actively satirised by the Eagle, who spends a good deal of wit upon his helpless passenger. From his remarks we learn how the dreamer, determined to serve Venus and Cupid despite his own failure in love, has devoted his meagre abilities to producing every kind of literary compliment to the god. As a painfully ungifted writer who knows nothing at first hand about the central topic of poetry, the dreamer is doubly comic; and the Eagle's account of him struggling with a task which makes

> A-nyght ful oft thyn hed to ake
> In thy studye, so thou writest,   [HF 632–3

does not reduce the absurdity of his character. His dedication appears still more ridiculous when the Eagle reveals how ignorant he is about the subject which he is continually celebrating in verse. 'Thou hast no tydynges', the Eagle mocks,

> Of Loves folk yf they be glade,
> Ne of noght elles that God made;   [HF 645-6

a remark which seems to confirm that the desert, empty of everything 'yformed by Nature', represents the dry sterility of the dreamer's restricted experience. 'And noght oonly fro fer contree,' the Eagle continues unkindly,

> That ther no tydynge cometh to thee,
> But of thy verray neyghebores,
> That duellen almost at thy dores,
> Thou herist neyther that ne this.
>
> [HF 648-51

As he continues his remarks Chaucer is probably parodying his own existence as a customs official, who after the 'rekenynges' of his daily records goes home to an evening absorbed in his books, as though deliberately avoiding contact with everyday life. 'For when thy labour doon al ys,' the Eagle goes on,

> And hast mad alle thy rekenynges,
> In stede of reste and newe thynges
> Thou goost hom to thy hous anoon;
> And, also domb as any stoon,
> Thou sittest at another book
> Tyl fully daswed ys thy look,
> And lyvest thus as an heremyte,
> Although thyn abstynence ys lyte.
>
> [HF 653-60

We might believe that during the period of his controllership Chaucer lived a double life, divided between his professional activities and a growing private library, but not that his duties kept him chained to a desk and endless book-keeping.[1] By

---

[1] It was, however, a condition of his appointment that he should write his rolls in his own hand.

satirising the scholarly impulse in his temperament, and saying nothing about his comprehensive experience as courtier, diplomat and civil servant, Chaucer produces a comic caricature of himself – not sparing an allusion to his waistline – which deepens the joke of his helpless situation. But the passage shows the dreamer to be a sufficiently comic figure without this additional absurdity. Although aspiring to serve the god of Love as a poet – a vocation for a courtier, not for a ledger-clerk – he lives in such hermitlike retirement, lost in the books which protect him from everyday reality, that he lacks even a rudimentary knowledge of the subject which he constantly writes about.

When the Eagle refers to this subject as 'Loves folk' he seems to be promising the dreamer a typical courtly vision, culminating in a more respectful picture of romantic love than Book I provides. In fact Chaucer does not return to this topic in *The Hous of Fame*, and 'Loves folk' prove to be not the figures of a courtly ideal but a much more plebeian crowd drawn from common life. This might be foreseen in the Eagle's promise of the 'wonder thynges' awaiting the dreamer at the end of his flight, where he will hear

> of Loves folk moo tydynges
> Both sothe sawes and lesinges;
> And moo loves newe begonne,
> And longe yserved loves wonne,
> And moo loves casuelly
> That ben betyd, no man wot why,
> But as a blynd man stert an hare;
> And more jolitee and fare
> Whil that they finde love of stel,
> As thinketh hem, and over-al wel . . .
> And moo berdys in two houres
> · Withouten rasour or sisoures
> Ymad, then greynes be of sondes.

[HF 675–91

Some parts of this prospect, like the reference to 'longe yserved loves wonne', are compatible with the terms of *fine amour*, but the

vigorously colloquial tone of the speech does not suggest that the
dreamer is being carried towards the fantasies of a love-vision.
Nor does the Eagle's promise imply much reverence for love.
Speaking of passionate involvements which came about quite
by chance, 'as a blynd man sterte an hare', he finds a graphic
simile to represent his robustly realistic attitude; and his sar-
donic comment about those who think they have found themselves a 'love of stel' should remind us of Dido's scepticism over
lovers' oaths. Again, his reference to the credulous lovers whose
beards are made 'withouten rasour or sisoures' – meaning that
they are duped – treats love as human absurdity, and supports
the narrator's refusal to enthuse over Dido as a romantic figure
in Book I. When the dreamer reaches his promised destination,
to be staggered by the ceaseless outpourings of 'tydynges' from
the House of Rumour, even these commonplace aspects of love
fail to materialise. Instead of lovers, the folk who crowd the
whirling house are couriers, shipmen, travellers, messengers and
gossips: a host of wildly animated talkers and story-tellers who
display no special concern with love, but discuss every conceivable topic bearing on human affairs. If Chaucer always had
this end in mind, the phrase 'Loves folk' is not to be understood
in its obvious sense of those devoted to romantic love or *fine
amour*; and we may ask whether he is exploiting the less immediate association of Venus with poetry – not only the writing
which honours the goddess by showing the power of passionate
love, but of all poetry impelled by her creative force. It is Venus
to whom the dreamer of *The Parlement of Foules* appeals for
'myght to ryme and ek t'endyte'; and although he can properly
expect her patronage when love is his subject, as in this work,
the goddess seems to have a general concern with imaginative
literature whatever its interests. In *The Hous of Fame* 'Loves
folk' are clearly not lovers, courtly or plebeian, but people of all
kinds brought into existence by the dream. This means, we
might say, that they are creatures of the poet's imagination,
though at this point of the dream the dreamer is still incapable
of creating such figures.

Meanwhile, before he acquires this power, the dreamer is

given a vastly increased awareness of the world about him,
which hitherto he has hardly explored further than his own
doorstep. Plucked out of his hermit-crab existence, he is carried
upwards to a point high above the earth from which he gazes
down upon whole continents and seas. Directed by the Eagle, he
looks down and picks out fields and plains,

> And now hilles, and now mountaynes,
> Now valeyes, now forestes,
> And now unnethes grete bestes;
> Now ryveres, now citees,
> Now tounes, and now grete trees,
> Now shippes seyllynge in the see.   [HF 898–903

In its range and scope the dreamer's view has become as unlimited as the mural painting which he had found so astonishing.
Through this panoramic view of the earth he now shares with
the unknown artist the broad vision which takes in the whole
field of human experience, and grasps the hidden principles by
which life is created and shaped. As the Eagle rises still higher,
the dreamer sees the beginnings of the natural forces which
eventually determine the kinds of weather:

> Tho gan y loken under me
> And beheld the ayerissh bestes,
> Cloudes, mystes, and tempestes,
> Snowes, hayles, reynes, wyndes,
> And th'engendrynge in hir kyndes,
> Al the wey thurgh which I cam.
> 'O God!' quod y, 'that made Adam,
> Moche ys thy myght and thy noblesse!'
>   [HF 964–71

This privileged view of natural 'engendrynge' gives the dreamer
some understanding of the vital process of which the poet's making is another form: an understanding necessary to successful
creation in art. Such a wonderful adventure must seem appropriate to a dream, but the fact that the dreamer is an aspiring
poet whose work suffers from his lack of common experience and
over-dependence on books gives his celestial flight a particular

importance. From the Eagle's remarks about 'tydynges' it appears that he cannot pursue his craft successfully unless he knows human character minutely and at first hand, and has the same familiarity with the circumstances of human life. What the dreamer sees of man's setting from the air – the towns, forests, mountains, plains, great rivers – provides one vital part of this creative understanding. The other essential, a broad knowledge of human nature and temperament, is promised when the Eagle delivers him to the destination where his comically persistent efforts to write poetry will be rewarded.

'Fames Hous', the Eagle explains in a long scientific discourse during their flight, is the collecting-point of every word spoken, whispered or sung on earth. As ripples move across the surface of water, sound travels in vibrations through air. Since every creature and object, as Aristotle argues, is urged by natural inclination towards its 'proper mansyon', where it is most at home, it follows that sound obeys the same impulse to find its natural resting-place; and this, the Eagle declares, brings every earthly noise to the house which they are soon to reach:

> every speche of every man . . .
> Moveth up on high to pace
> Kyndely to Fames place.   [HF 849–52

At the end of his journey the dreamer will be able to listen to every conversation and remark, public or private, as it occurs on earth. The importance of this experience for a poet who spends his life in hermit-like seclusion, 'domb as any stoon', hardly needs to be explained. Just as his physical horizon has been dramatically expanded by his flight above the earth, so his scanty knowledge of human affairs will be hugely increased by the special privilege which enables him to overhear every plea, argument, discussion or blandishment uttered on earth, as invisible audience. The familiarity with every kind of temperament which he will derive from this unlimited eavesdropping will be supplemented by a second 'wonder thyng'. Just before

leaving the dreamer to explore Fame's House, the Eagle
explains that as each utterance reaches this palace of noise it
assumes the appearance of its speaker;

> And hath so verray hys lyknesse
> That spak the word, that thou wilt gesse
> That it the same body be.

[HF 1079–81

The dreamer will hear the voice, and simultaneously see an
image of its owner. Although these figures will be fantasmal,
they will appear indistinguishable from the folk whom the
dreamer might see about him in everyday life, were he not
absorbed in his books. In this respect there seems nothing
wonderful about his experience. Its marvellous quality lies in
the way it will connect private conversation and habits of speech
with a particular face, teaching the dreamer how to discern
individual nature in physical features, dress and gesture. *The
General Prologue* shows to what use a poet might put such awareness. The fantasmal beings who are to bring the poet 'tydynges'
of the world beyond his doors are suggestively akin to the creatures of imagination, who although fictional have the living
authenticity of actual men and women, seen with the sharp
particularity which is a measure of the poet's creative energy.
Here the dreamer might find reason for astonishment, in discovering that disembodied voices could take shapes and names,
to exist as creatures independent of the poet and seemingly as
substantial as the men and women who inhabit the world of
waking truth.

As they approach the end of their journey, the Eagle draws
the dreamer's attention to the 'grete swogh' that rumbles up and
down inside the celestial building; and once again the dreamer
is deafened by a noise great enough to shake any normal sleeper
out of his trance. 'Peter! lyk betynge of the see,' the dreamer
answers when he is asked for a comparison,

> 'ayen the roches holowe,
> Whan tempest doth the shippes swalowe . . .
> Or elles lyk the last humblynge

After the clappe of a thundringe,
Whan Joves hath the air ybete.'

[HF 1035–41

Loud and discordant noises have no proper place in a love-
vision, whose typical sounds are those of music, birdsong, warm
breezes and running water; but the raucous shouting and horn-
blowing which Chaucer forces upon the myth of Alcyone give
notice of an intention which persists unchecked in *The Hous of
Fame*. By discovering that the great building is reverberating
with thunderous 'tydynges' the dreamer indicates that his
experience is to be dominated by terrifyingly loud noises; and
also provides the first intimation that the title of the poem
involves a pun. Up to the end of Book I nothing suggests that
'fame' has any other sense than renown or the infamy which
Dido fears; and the reader probably supposes that the building
at the end of the dreamer's flight will prove to be a storehouse of
reputations, good and bad, earned by other famous characters.
But during his flight the dreamer learns from the Eagle that
the fame collected here is nothing more than noise, since

> every word that spoken ys
> Cometh into Fames Hous, ywys.   [HF 881–2

When he enters the building, however, it appears that the Eagle
had misled him. Instead of the personified 'tydynges' which he
has been warned to expect, he sees a vast assembly of coats-of-
arms representing

> famous folk that han ybeen
> In Auffrike, Europe, and Asye,
> Syth first began the chevalrie.   [HF 1338–40

In addition, much of the hall is occupied by statues of the poets
and chroniclers who have kept alive the fame of national heroes
and achievements. The dreamer recognises that he has not yet
reached the 'wonder thyng' promised by the Eagle, but when
he is guided to the House of Rumour he at last encounters
'Loves folk' and the source of the indescribable clamour which
makes him sweat for fear in the last moments of his flight. Since

'rumour' is one of the primary senses of the term which the whole poem takes as motif, and since 'fame' also has the sense of public report, common talk, or rumour,[1] to which the whirling house is devoted, a single concept appears to run through each of the poem's main developments, exploiting different aspects of the complex word used in its title.

By looking ahead to these later sequences of the story, we grasp the serious underlying purpose of the Eagle's learned discourse on sound, which at first reading seems entirely comic. The mock-scholarship of this lecture to a captive audience would earn a place in the poem simply by its solemn absurdity. 'Whan a pipe is blowen sharpe,' the Eagle explains to the dreamer,

> The air ys twyst with violence
> And rent; loo, thys ys my sentence:
> Eke, whan men harpe-strynges smyte,
> Whether hyt be moche or lyte,
> Loo, with the strok the ayr tobreketh;
> And ryght so breketh it when men speketh.
>
> [HF 775-80

The introduction of pipers and harpers early in Book III could make us suspect that the Eagle's argument has something more than a comic function: the lecture is now being illustrated by figures whose activity relates to a central idea of the poem. As the term 'fame' comes under imaginative pressure, its linked meanings find expression in images and verbal references to reputation, news, rumour and announcement, but especially to noise as the agency by which all these are broadcast or noised abroad. Among these related ideas, 'tydynges' begins to seem particularly important. When the term is first used, during the Eagle's criticism of the dreamer's self-isolated existence, it evidently means news or information, whose absence leaves the dreamer ignorant both of Love's folk and of the rest of creation. As a reward for his diligent service, he is to hear 'moo tydynges' of Love's folk than he could reckon in a lifetime. These must be

[1] See OED, *fame* 1.

the speeches and conversations which reach the Hous of Fame
in consequence of the natural law outlined by the Eagle,
though they are not limited to lovers' exchanges. It now becomes
clear that *The Hous of Fame* cannot be described as a love-
vision, for what the dreamer is to see at this universal collecting-
point of noise has no reference to any single human activity or
interest. The 'tydynges' of mixed humanity which the dreamer
hears long before reaching the Hous,

> Bothe of feir speche and chidynges,
> And of fals and soth compouned,   [HF 1028–9

could be described as 'fame' in the sense of common talk – 'that
which people say or tell'; and as these reports include falsehood
as well as truth, they may also be described as 'rumour' in its
modern and medieval sense. The relationship which brings
together 'fame', 'tydynges' and 'rumour' helps to emphasise the
poem's concern with noise in its many associations, from the
literal 'grete swogh' emitted by the Hous to the reports of Love's
folk without which the dreamer's poetry will remain lifeless.
Although seen initially as the kind of knowledge that is gained
by wide human experience, these 'tydynges' have a more specific
connection with the poet's creative power, and thus with his
literary fame, which is admitted later in the poem.

The notion of fame as celebrity or renown comes forward as
the dreamer takes stock of his new surroundings. The Hous is
built on a hill of ice, on whose slopes are inscribed the names of
those who have enjoyed fame, but many of them have melted
and become illegible. On the northern side, however,

> writen ful of names
> Of folkes that hadden grete fames
> Of olde tyme,   [HF 1153–5

the inscriptions remain as distinct as when they were cut. The
dreamer offers no comment on this arbitrary survival of reputation of which he is soon to see more; but turns his attention to
the beauty and marvellous craftsmanship of the building itself.
'Al the men that ben on lyve,' he declares,

Ne han the kunnynge to descrive
The beaute of that ylke place,
Ne coude casten no compace
Swich another for to make,
That myght of beaute ben hys make,
Ne so wonderlych ywrought.

[HF 1168–73

It is the 'grete craft' of the Hous rather than its physical beauty
which most impresses the dreamer: a quality displayed in its
structure 'withouten peces or joynynges', and in the many 'sub-
til compassinges' or decorative features which enrich its exterior:

Babewynnes and pynacles,
Ymageries and tabernacles
I say; and ful eke of wyndowes
As flakes falle in grete snowes.   [HF 1189–92

This recalls the architectural extravagance of the Temple of
Venus, a likeness which extends to the swarming profusion of
ornament and figures in both buildings. As the dreamer en-
thuses over this new master-work, describing the occupants of
the 'sondry habitacles' let into the walls, he is led back to his
major theme:

alle maner of mynstralles
And gestiours, that tellen tales
Both of wepinge and of game,
Of al that longeth unto Fame.

[HF 1197–1200

This function of spreading the renown of famous men reminds
us, not for the first time, that poets and story-tellers are responsible for keeping alive the fame of those who achieved celebrity
by their deeds, and that some of the heroic reputations which
their lays create are entirely fictional. The humblest of such
chroniclers, the 'smale harpers with her glees', occupy places
beneath the most eminent of their calling, trying to imitate their
greater skill; and standing apart from them are the more
accomplished musicians who perform at feasts and celebrations:

G

> That maden lowde mynstralcies
> In cornemuse and shalemyes,
> And many other maner pipe,
> That craftely begunne to pipe.   [HF 1217–20

Moving to another part of the hall, the dreamer sees players of more strident wind-instruments,

> hem that maken blody soun
> In trumpe, beme, and claryoun;   [HF 1239–40

among them some of the famous trumpeters of antiquity – Misenus, Joab, and Thiodamus, who was in fact a Theban augur and not a musician. In this respect Chaucer may have been at fault in associating him with the others, who are relevant to his theme both symbolically and by reason of the trumpeter's function of announcing great events and their performers. But the next group of figures, who share a common concern with prophesy, suggests that Thiodamus the augur is not entirely out of place:

> Magiciens, and tregetours,
> And Phitonesses, charmeresses,
> Olde wicches, sorceresses,
> That use exorsisacions,
> And eke these fumygacions;
> And clerkes eke, which konne wel
> Al this magik naturel.   [HF 1260–6

Unlike the others, these are not noise-makers, but by forecasting future events they can claim some association with the historians of the past whose statues stand inside the golden hall of Fames Hous. Their place in the poem is unambiguous. The first of these chroniclers, 'hym of secte saturnyn', is plainly identified as the writer responsible for the fame of Jewish military achievements:

> The Ebrayk Josephus, the olde,
> That of Jewes gestes tolde;
> And he bar on his shuldres hye
> The fame up of the Jewerye.   [HF   1433–6

Statius is similarly honoured, as the historian who gave renown
to Thebes and to the deeds of Achilles; and beside him a group
of writers – among them Homer, Guido delle Colonne, and
Geoffrey of Monmouth – are commemorated for their part in
perpetuating the fame of Troy. Virgil appears next, as author
of the epic poem which has sustained the famous name of
'Pius Eneas' for so long. Then, after referring to the reputations,
national and personal, kept alive by Ovid, Lucan and Claudian,
the dreamer abandons his attempt to list all the chroniclers
represented there, remarking picturesquely that the building
was as full of the authors of 'olde gestes'

As ben on trees rokes nestes;   [HF 1516

a comparison which renews the sense of contact with everyday
reality.

During this long description the dreamer does not remind us
that he is himself an aspiring poet, though his familiarity with so
many authors proves the scholarly impulse which hitherto has
absorbed all his free time. The crowd of figures on the façade of
the Hous and inside all bear upon this private interest, by representing the means by which great historical events and persons
are given lasting fame, whether in epic verse or in the song of a
local minstrel. The fact that the writers and singers of such
heroic tales have honourable places in the hall of the Hous
recognises that some chroniclers can make themselves as famous
as the achievements which they keep alive. But the dreamer
does not pause over this fact, or express any hope that his own
writing may bring him fame. What he sees of the unjust and
capricious treatment meted out by the goddess of Fame to her
suppliants makes his silence appear well-advised. The first
group, seeking reward for actions which deserve to be remembered, is dismissed out of hand upon an arbitrary impulse. 'For
me ne lyst hyt noght,' the goddess declares,

No wyght shal speke of yow, ywis,
Good ne harm, ne that ne this.   [HF 1565–6

A second group, also hoping to win renown by their virtuous

deeds, are still more unfortunate. Instead of the good name they
deserve, the goddess promises them the reputation of evil-doers:

> Y graunte yow
> That ye shal have a shrewed fame,
> And wikkyd loos, and worse name,
> Though ye good loos have wel deserved.
>
> [HF 1618–21

Although the suppliants of the next group are more generously
treated, their reward is no more just than the others, for to spite
their enemies the goddess gives them more fame than they
deserve. Towards the fourth group she is more compliant. Their
good acts have been prompted by love of virtue, not of fame,
and they have no wish to be remembered. 'Hyde our werkes and
our name,' they plead, and the goddess grants their request
without more ado; but when a fifth group makes the same plea
to be forgotten, explaining that

> they yeven noght a lek
> For fame ne for such renoun,   [HF 1708–9

the goddess treats the suggestion as an affront to common justice
and to her own dignity. 'And be ye wood?' she demands angrily,

> And wene ye for to doo good,
> And for to have of that no fame?
> Have ye dispit to have my name?
> Ne, ye shul lyven everychon!   [HF 1714–17

This inconstancy of attitude is displayed again when the next two
groups supplicate for the same favour. Although both have been
too lazy and comfort-loving to stir themselves to any worthy
endeavour, they ask the goddess to give them the fame of men
who have 'doon noble gestes' and distinguished themselves in
love. Coming from one group, the request is well received, but
when the other repeats it the goddess maliciously promises to
make the suppliants infamous throughout the world. She is
equally severe in relying to the next request, presented by a
party of traitors and wicked wrongoers who beg for an honour-

able reputation; but when a second group of criminals asks for the notoriety they deserve –

> That oure fame such be knowe
> In alle thing ryght as hit ys   [HF 1836–7

– she adopts an impartial position and promises them a truthful report. Among them is a criminal who in his hunger for celebrity set fire to an Athenian temple, seeing this as the only means by which he could become famous. 'As gret a fame han shrewes,' he tells the goddess,

> Though hit be for shrewednesse,
> As goode folk han for godnesse;   [HF 1853–4

and since one was out of reach he determined to have the other. The goddess applauds his decision, and orders her trumpeter to publish the news of his crime throughout the world.

The activities of Fame's court take up some three hundred lines of the poem without much developing the imaginative interests previously introduced. As the dreamer himself remarks, although wonderful in itself this display of the arbitrary working of Fame is not what he came to see; and the reader might object that Chaucer is digressing from his complex central theme merely to exploit its most obvious association. The trumpetings of Eolus give Chaucer an opportunity of returning to a motif stated earlier in Book II, and impressively realised in his description of the curious building which the dreamer is next to see, whose overwhelming noise and rapidity of movement leave him stunned. The sound of the brazen trumpet, the dreamer comments, 'as al the world shulde overthrowe', rushed through every country

> As swifte as pelet out of gonne,
> Whan fyr is in the poudre ronne.   [HF 1643–4

But the procession of suppliants seems irrelevant to Chaucer's imaginative purpose, and the episode which follows reminds us not only of the 'newe tydynges' which the dreamer had been promised, but also of the particular interests which the poem had been following previously. As he watches the goddess

passing judgement, the dreamer is addressed by a man standing
behind him, who asks his name and enquires whether he too has
come to the Hous to acquire fame. The dreamer denies any
such intention. He will be satisfied, he explains modestly, to
remain unknown; and as though this attitude was determined
by his conception of the artist's function he adds:

> I wot myself best how y stonde;
> For what I drye, or what I thynke,
> I wil myselven al hyt drynke,
> Certeyn, for the more part,
> As fer forth as I kan myn art.
>
> [HF 1878–82

The exact sense of this remark is made obscure by the figurative
'drynke', which may allude to a proverbial expression, but evidently the dreamer is suggesting that he intends to be as self-
effacing in his poetry as in his private life; using art to conceal
personal feelings rather than making them his subject-matter.
This reference to the creative task brings Chaucer back to an
earlier preoccupation of *The Hous of Fame*, and with this realign-
ment of interest the dreamer too picks up the forgotten thread
of his adventure. His reason for visiting the Hous, he tells his
new acquaintance, was to learn

> Some newe thynges, y not what,
> Tydynges, other this or that,
> Of love, or suche thynges glade.   [HF 1887–9

The judgements of Fame certainly do not fit this description,
but his companion recognises what he was expecting to find,
and leads him to another and still more astonishing building at
the foot of the hill. The dreamer is again struck by the marvellous craftsmanship of the builder, surpassing even

> that Domus Dedaly,
> That Laboryntus cleped ys,[1]   [HF 1920–1

[1] The labyrinth of Daedalus is mentioned in *Boece*, iii. pr. 2, 'so entre-
laced that it is unable to ben unlaced'. Chaucer appears to have supposed
that the building had an interwoven structure rather than an intricate
ground-plan.

but what most astonishes him about this 'queynte hous' is its spinning movement. Unlike the Temple of Venus or the richly decorated building which he has just left, this wonderful struc-ture is woven out of twigs like a basket, and whirls round like a top to the accompaniment of a shattering barrage of noise. The dreamer has reached the destination promised by the Eagle, and the point of his dream where his ability to translate out-landish experience into poetry will be most searchingly tested. As he rises to this challenge, the poem begins to pulsate with a new sense of energy and excitement:

> That, for the swough and for the twygges,
> This hous was also ful of gygges,
> And also ful eke of chirkynges
> And of many other werkynges;
> And eke this hous hath of entrees
> As fele as of leves ben in trees
> In somer, whan they grene been.
>
> [HF 1941–7

The verse movement matches the noisy activity of the house, spinning 'as swyft as thought' and squeaking and twittering throughout its basketlike structure. A modern reader, more familiar than Chaucer with rapid motion and the noise of machines, may think his rotating house odd rather than impressive; but the poem is now generating an excitement which gives this culminating wonder a deep sense of actuality. How-ever unlikely the machine itself, the description of its rushing energy and tumultous noise create the experience for the reader, as the lines beat out an inexhaustible catalogue of the 'tydynges' which burst from the house as it spins tirelessly round:

> Of werres, of pes, of mariages,
> Of reste, of labour, of viages,
> Of abood, of deeth, of lyf,
> Of love, of hate, acord, of stryf . . .
> Of dyvers transmutacions
> Of estats, and eke of regions;
> Of trust, of drede, of jelousye,
> Of wit, of wynnynge, of folye,

Of plente, and of gret famyne,
Of chepe, of derthe, and of ruyne,
Of good or mysgovernement,
Of fyr, and of dyvers accident.
[HF 1961–4, 1969–76

This list does not conform exactly with the news promised by
the Eagle, but such a comprehensive survey of human affairs is
obviously the missing element of the dreamer's education. In its
diversity and breadth, which takes in far more than the stereo-
typed activities of courtly love, the great outpouring of 'tydynges' has a good deal in common with the epic work studied
by the dreamer at the beginning of his adventure. Both refuse to
be limited to particular areas of human experience, depicting
every aspect of man's emotional life and showing his subjection
to natural and political forces. Unlike the Virgilian mural,
however, the mass of impressions which deafen the dreamer are
shapeless and disorganised, the mere raw materials of a poem
which he has still to write. The vast human subject is being
presented to him simply in terms of sound, and with no pictorial counterpart such as the Eagle had described. The sheer
noisiness of the poem must again strike us, and remind us of the
previous associations of 'fame' with the outbursts of clamour
which have stunned the dreamer at various points of his adventure, now culminating in the incoherent din which could be
heard across two countries. Chaucer has returned to the tacit
reminder that if a man is to be famous, his acts must be noised
abroad: 'fame' is noise, and noising – whether by minstrel, epic
poet or common talk – is a necessary condition of acquiring
renown. The story of Aeneas retold in the temple, whose artis-
try makes a comic contrast with the dreamer's gauche attempts
to write, shows the craftsmanship by which the greatest reputations are created and kept alive. In addition, it reveals the extent
to which the poet depends upon the kind of 'tydynges' which the
dreamer is now encountering for the first time.

This reading of *The Hous of Fame* suggests that Chaucer is
writing not a love-vision but a poem closely concerned with the
nature of literature, and in particular with the kind of creative

activity which poetry involves. The narrator of *The Boke of the Duchesse* may be an unsuccessful lover, but we are not encouraged to think of him as an incompetent poet. In the narrator of his second dream-poem Chaucer develops a comic figure which persists in his later work, but this absurdly untalented character is not devised simply for comic effect. His ignorance of common life justifies the introduction of themes and ideas crucial to the imaginative purposes of *The Hous of Fame*: the epic masterpiece of Book I, the commemorative statues of poets and chroniclers who have perpetuated famous events, the blowing abroad of Fame's judgements, and the ambiguous 'tydynges' presented to the dreamer as reward for his services to the god of Love. However different in themselves, all these elements of the story are related to the central issue of creative activity: a concern about which the narrator speaks directly in the Proem to Book 2, when he calls upon the faculties of 'thought' and 'engyn' to render his dream into poetry. This, the Eagle will explain, he is unable to do while he remains ignorantly cut off from the 'tydynges' that are essential to the poet's art. When he reaches the whirling house of twigs, describing it as

> the moder of tydynges,
> As the see of welles and of sprynges,
>
> [HF 1983-4

the dreamer has arrived at the vital experience promised to him as poet.

The importance of what he will learn from this original source of news and information is revealed when the Eagle rejoins the dreamer, and answers his curiosity by picking him up and setting him inside the great spinning hive of noise. This action fulfils the Eagle's intention towards the dreamer, to

> wisse and teche the aryght
> Where thou maist most tidynges here,
>
> [HF 2024-5

in the most literal sense; for the dreamer finds the building crammed with the largest crowd of people ever seen, all

ceaselessly gossiping and multiplying rumours. 'Every wight
that I saugh there,' the dreamer reports,

> Rouned everych in others ere,
> A newe tydynge prively,
> Or elles tolde al openly
> Ryght thus, and seyde: 'Nost not thou
> That ys betyd, lo, late or now?'
> 'No,' quod he, 'telle me what.'
> And than he tolde hym this and that.
>
> [HF 2044-50

As gossip is passed from mouth to mouth fresh details are added,
and the reports grow large enough to fly out of one of the
numerous windows of the house; the true sometimes in company with the false, and swearing never to be separated. What
the dreamer now sees inside the House of Rumour does not
match the Eagle's forecast about the activities of 'Loves folk'
that would be shown to him; nor does he seem particularly
impressed by anything he hears. Outside, the unearthly din
produced by the 'chirkynges' of the basket-built house com-
bined with the chattering of its unseen occupants makes it
impossible to distinguish any single remark; inside, what strikes
the dreamer is the speed and energy with which rumours spring
up and develop. 'Were the tydynge soth or fals,' he remarks,

> Yit wolde he telle hyt natheles,
> And evermo with more encres
> Than yt was erst. Thus north and south
> Wente every tydynge fro mouth to mouth,
> And that encresing ever moo,
> As fyr ys wont to quyke and goo
> From a spark spronge amys,
> Til al a citee brent up ys.
>
> [HF 2073-80

The dreamer is not only being allowed to listen to universal
gossip, but is learning how 'tydynges' originate inside the building whose whirling motion offers a parallel to the tireless
rumour-mongering of its myriad inhabitants. The openness of

the house, whose doors and windows stand ajar day and night, with no porter to hinder comings and goings, complements the sleepless activity of its occupants. Their continuous rumour-making has the character of a simple creative process; and if it is right to see a persistent concern with poetic creation in *The Hous of Fame*, it would follow that where the dreamer reaches the end of his journey, Chaucer arrives at his own imaginative destination. The spinning House of Rumour, ceaselessly alert to new reports, making and propagating true and false 'tydynges' inside the humming contrivance 'shapen lyk a cage', truly embodies such a climax of discovery, for in this tireless generating of news and report Chaucer represents the working of the creative imagination; the 'engyn' of the Proem to Book II. It is typical of his punning on key words of this poem that 'engyn' should also signify, for the medieval as for the modern reader, the kind of mechanical device through which Chaucer has expressed awareness of his own creative activity.

With this understanding of their source, the term 'tydynges' assumes a new significance within the poem. What initially determines the poet's ability as maker is not the extent of his human experience, which the Eagle enlarges so dramatically, but the strength of the imaginative impulse which provides the driving energy of the poem and its design. This shaping conception reaches the poet as 'tydynges' in two senses of the word, for besides indicating report or rumour the term also means a happening or event.[1] Such a happening is the experience commonly described as inspiration, in which the poet not only finds sentences forming and gathering together as though implanted in his mind without his assistance, but sees the fictional characters and events of his poem presenting themselves with the force of actual happenings. The strength of such imaginative presentation is well suggested by the Eagle when he describes how the 'tydynges' arriving at the Hous will not only manifest themselves as noise, but take on the lifelike appearance of their speakers. The dreamer readily agrees that this is 'a wonder thyng'; and

[1] See OED *tiding*, 1; with an illustration taken from *MLT* 628: 'How that this blisful tidyng is bifalle.'

not for the last time in *The Hous of Fame* this conventional attribute of a dream is applied to a characteristic aspect of the
creative process.

The vast crowd of folk which the dreamer joins inside the
House of Rumour represents the personified 'tydynges' which
he has been warned to expect, though with one feature which
might not have been predicted. The great company is almost
exclusively lower-class, consisting in large part of shipmen, pilgrims with 'scrippes bret-ful of lesinges', pardoners, couriers and
messengers. Although not at all suggestive of Love's folk in the
courtly associations of the term, they are all in their own way
story-tellers, and to this extent subjects of Venus in her special
concern with literary creation. As every commentator notices,
Chaucer seems to be feeling his way towards the more famous
group of pilgrims with stories to tell, who are the joint narrators
of his final work. The likeness extends to the boisterous vitality
of the figures in the House of Rumour, embodied from the
'tydynges' which it generates. In their struggle for precedence
at the windows they anticipate the quarrelsome self-assertive-
ness of the Canterbury pilgrims, and especially of the churls
who refuse to recognise the need for an orderly succession of
tales:

> so they gonne crowde,
> Til ech of hem gan crien lowde,
> 'Lat me go first!' 'Nay, but let me!'
>
> [HF 2095-7

In this final episode of the poem, with its impression of noisy
confusion and the predominance of plebeian manners, the world
of common affairs breaks in upon Chaucer's poetry in earnest.
There have been strong hints of this development earlier in the
story. Book I treats a theme of courtly romance mainly from the
position of realistic bourgeois judgement; and the Eagle, whose
familiar manner and *bonhomie* foreshadow the personal qualities
of the pilgrims' innkeeper guide, carries the poem decisively away
from courtly formality and towards the untidy exuberance of
natural impulse. The poem ends with another outburst of noisy

energy that cannot be controlled by formal discipline, though
with a half-promise that some form of order is about to be im-
posed upon the unruly mob of rumour-makers. As the dreamer
watches the mass of gossip and false report being propagated, he
hears an explosion of noise from a corner of the hall

> Ther men of love-tydynges tolde,   [HF 2143

and sees all the occupants of the house running towards it,
questioning each other about this sudden development. In
crowding together, struggling for a view of whatever is happening, they embody again the unruly wildness and confusion
which lie furthest from the serenely ordered presentation of a
courtly ideal:

> And whan they were alle on an hepe,
> Tho behynde begunne up lepe,
> And clamben up on other faste,
> And up the nose and yen kaste,
> And troden faste on others heles,
> And stampen, as men doon aftir eles.
>
> [HF 2149–54

The squabbling turmoil of the scene has several counterparts in
Chaucer's later work, with a close parallel in *The Parlement of
Foules* when the impatient lower-class birds threaten to break up
the meeting in disorder; but there as in other poems the
rebellious impulse is held in check by the personal authority of
a figure who is recognised as ruler or arbitrator. Such a figure is
glimpsed in the closing lines of The Hous of Fame, before the
narrative breaks off without explanation:

> Atte laste y saugh a man
> Which that y nevene nat ne kan,
> But he semed for to be
> A man of gret auctorite.   [HF 2155–8

The traditional suggestions that this unidentified newcomer
must be John of Gaunt or some other historical personage have
no possible imaginative basis. If he is a meaningful figure, the
'man of gret auctorite' whom the dreamer is either unwilling or

unable to name must be accountable in terms which the poem
itself proposes, and which satisfy the logic of its development.
So far as that development has followed a concern with the
creative process, it is proper to see the newcomer embodying a
vital impulse in the making of a poem. Although the dreamer
may not wish to identify him, the function of his 'gret auctorite'
within the context of the poem is not difficult to infer. The
undisciplined crowd of gossips and rumour-mongers, endlessly
repeating stories about every kind of human activity, provide
the raw material of poetry; in itself indispensable, as the Eagle
has made the dreamer realise, but needing firm and purposeful
organisation if its vital energies are to serve the poet. As this
mass of ideas and figures poured out by imagination represents
part of his creative activity, so does the force of authority which
shapes and controls this undirected impulse into the intelligible
patterns of art. Creation is inseparable from the critical instinct
of the artist, who must discipline expression into a mould determined by him, and not allow his creatures to seize power themselves. Had Chaucer been a contemporary of Coleridge he
might have written explicitly on the creative working of imagination. Being a medieval poet, he made *The Hous of Fame*
express his awareness of this crucial process in a manner typical
of his art: through metaphors of celestial flight, a whirling
house, a gabbling multitude, and the figure of authority who
arrives at the point where Chaucer finds it impossible, or
unnecessary, to continue the exploration of his creative consciousness.

Chaucer's awareness of the working of imagination is more
remarkable in its recognition of a process so little reflected upon
by medieval philosophy that no adequate terminology was
available to him. As we have seen, when the dreamer invokes
his creative powers in the Proem to Book II, using the imprecise
term 'thought', he indicates the vagueness of medieval thinking
about the process involved. But Chaucer at least realises that
both the original 'drem' and the 'engyn' required to describe
this private experience are functions of his own mind; and the
striking metaphors by which he represents the working of

imagination show his understanding of the power-house upon which his poetry depended. By writing his discovery into *The Hous of Fame* Chaucer suggests its importance to him as a poet. To understand the nature and behaviour of the creative consciousness, or at least to be familiar with its activity, is a stage of poetic development as vital as becoming widely acquainted with human character, or reaching critical awareness of the standards of great art. Each of these necessary achievements is recognised in *The Hous of Fame*, and the first of them – though perhaps not predictably – provides the imaginative terminus of the poem. When the narrative breaks off, Chaucer has just introduced the final element in the complex creative 'engyn' which makes him a poet. It is difficult to see how he could go further without making his underlying purpose explicit; and difficult to resist the inference that at this point, where the inner significance of his metaphor was about to disclose itself, Chaucer found himself unwilling to continue the story.

A considered judgement of *The Hous of Fame* is likely to retain the impression of an imperfectly unified structure which a first reading conveys. Although Book I is joined to the others by several common ideas, they are not sufficiently powerful to link this section of the dream to its sequel with any convincing consequence, or to give inevitability to the poet's design. There seems no compelling reason why the dreamer's adventure should begin in the Temple of Venus, or why Dido should occupy so conspicuous a place in this opening phase of a dream which then ignores love. The theme of personal fame which relates her story to later interests of the poem is introduced without emphasis; and without the title of the poem to suggest its importance we should not expect to find the idea developed in Books II and III. A reader may feel that Chaucer embarked on this second dream-poem with no very definite notion of where the story was to carry him; ready to explore side-roads and footpaths somewhat at random to the point where, with the help of the dreamer's nameless acquaintance, the poem is directed firmly towards the disclosure which at last fulfils the promise made by the Eagle some fifteen hundred lines earlier.

Variations in the poetic depth of the poem suggest how uneven his commitment was. His account of Fame arbitrarily awarding her favours is allegorical writing without surprises, which interrupts the dreamer's search to no useful purpose. The description of creative activity inside the house where all 'tydynges' originate, on the other hand, uses the suggestive power of poetry to represent Chaucer's intuitive knowledge of the imaginative process, which he would perhaps have been unable to communicate in any other way. By leaving his account of this culminating wonder unfinished, he gives the sense of purposeless meandering its final confirmation: at last even he, it might seem, exhausts his appetite for astonishing oddity. In fact, like the dreamer, he has reached his destination; not by the quickest route, but with a final certainty of understanding which makes amends for the sightseeing ruminations along the way.

IV

THE PARLEMENT OF FOULES

THE third and most accomplished of Chaucer's dream-poems takes the reader through an experience already partly familiar from the two previous works. The opening stanzas introduce a narrator who disclaims any special knowledge of love, a subject which he knows only by report, and who relies upon books for most of his knowledge of human affairs. Like his counterpart in *The Hous of Fame* he is an assiduous reader, who loses himself for a whole day in an absorbed study of the book 'write with lettres olde' which partly motivates his dream. Like the romance chosen by the narrator of *The Boke of the Duchesse*, the book contains an account of a marvellous vision, and has the same kind of influence over his sleeping mind. In his dream he is guided by another imposing figure, who treats him with much the same amused disrespect as the previous dreamer suffers in the Eagle's claws, chaffing him about his ignorance and timidity, but genially promising him 'mater of to wryte' as a reward for his literary enterprise. Again like the Eagle, Africanus acts as guide only until the dreamer has reached the threshold of this promised revelation, and then leaves him to provide his own interpretation of what he sees and hears. The garden in which the dreamer finds himself is the most familiar of settings, many of whose features had appeared in *The Boke of the Duchesse*. But now, although finding hints of melancholy and suicidal frenzy in the romantic figures which decorate another temple of Venus, instead of a self-isolated mourner the dreamer encounters the goddess of natural creation, thronged round by the great assembly she has called together to begin another generative cycle on St Valentine's Day.

Points of similarity between *The Parlement of Foules* and the two other dream-poems seem not to offer much help in assessing

Chaucer's purposes in this puzzling work. Unlike *The Hous of Fame*, it seems at first to fit happily inside the category of love-vision, for except during his recapitulation of the *Somnium Scipionis* the dreamer is almost continuously concerned with aspects of love and marriage. But we have already seen that the associations of love in Chaucer's early poetry are often ambiguous, and it is not always clear what intention he gives his references to this important topic. The blissful lady Cytherea,

> That with thy fyrbrond dauntest whom the lest,   [PF 114

obviously initiates the impulse of sexual love; but by appealing to her for 'myght to ryme and ek t'endyte', the narrator shows that she also provides the inspiration of poetry. The same ambiguity of purpose seems to be half admitted in the opening sentence of *The Parlement*, when after alluding to the brevity of life and the endless requirements of 'the craft', the narrator adds the helpful clarification,

> Al this mene I by love.   [PF 4

Perhaps he does, but the remark seems ironically calculated, as though intended to mislead the unwary reader rather than to enlighten him. The lines remind us of the craftsmanship painfully acquired by the poet, as well as of the conventions to be observed by the lover; and this hint of Chaucer's double purposes runs forward through the poem, warning us against a reading which sees *The Parlement* simply as a love-vision. If it does not seem a very complex poem at first reading, that may be because Chaucer has now acquired an ability for which 'craft' is the appropriate term.

The obvious difficulty of *The Parlement of Foules* lies in the inconclusive ending, which denies us any purposeful resolution of the issues which the poem proposes. The tacit conflict between the forces represented by Nature and Venus, if this is accepted, remains undetermined when the parliament disperses. So too does the matter of the formel eagle's choice of mate, and the noisy argument between the various kinds of bird over the appropriate behaviour of a lover has no settled outcome. As the great assembly breaks up, its questions unanswered, the dreamer wakes; not relieved and re-established by his experience, as his counterpart in *The Boke of the Duchesse* is cured of depression by his meeting with suicidal melancholy, but still searching for the answer to his unstated question, which he may find in some other book:

> I wok, and othere bokes tok me to,
> To reede upon, and yit I rede alwey.   [PF 695–6

Before the dream begins, he is eager to study the *Somnium Scipionis* in the hope that it may yield some positive information, 'a certeyn thyng', about which he is not specific. The poem ends without representing any such discovery, and without any such culminating event as the disclosure of the knight's loss in *The Boke of the Duchesse*, or the appearance of the man of great authority at the point where *The Hous of Fame* breaks off. The roundel sung by the birds at their departure brings *The Parlement* to a harmonious close, but without disguising the fact that the poem's questions have been shelved and not solved. Like the formel eagle's suitors, the reader is left only with an indefinite suggestion that the problems will perhaps be settled at some later date; and with an impression that the narrator is continuing his search for the truth which has eluded him:

> I hope, ywis, to rede so som day
> That I shal mete som thyng for to fare
> The bet, and thus to rede I nyl nat spare.   [PF 697–9

But neither the inconclusiveness of the debate, whether between the rival positions of Venus and Nature or the excitable birds, nor the dreamer's attempt to resolve his undefined problem, is reflected in the shaping and expression of this assured poem. In compactness and sense of controlled purpose *The Parlement* seems to be a more deeply considered work than either of its predecessors, and is technically much more accomplished. The change from octosyllabic couplets to rhyme royal indicates Chaucer's greater confidence in his craftsmanship, for a much tighter discipline is needed to accommodate ideas to this more

complex form; but he handles his new medium with an ease
which makes his stanza seem ideally suited to continuous narrative. His certainty of touch makes it difficult to suppose that the
unresolved ending of the story represents a failure to work out
its imaginative interests. It seems better to assume that the
inconclusive terminus of *The Parlement* is part of its poetic
design, a condition of the poem bound up with its meaning; for
meaning is not separable from the terms in which the poet
presents his experience. It may be helpful to begin an examina-
tion of *The Parlement* by scrutinising one of its persistent figures –
that of the conflict of attitudes which is seen most plainly in the
bird's debate.

The poem prepares us for this conflict from the outset. What
the dreamer reveals of himself in the opening stanzas, as an
aspirant who knows about love from books but 'nat in dede',
suggests no reason for melancholy; and in speaking of his discovery of the *Somnium Scipionis* he describes his positive excitement:

> To rede forth hit gan me so delite
> That al that day me thoughte but a lyte.
>
> [PF 27–8

Yet at the end of this absorbing day the dreamer admits himself
depressed and preoccupied, 'fulfyld of thought and busy hevynesse', as though something found in his reading were troubling
him; perhaps by reminding him of private difficulties about
which he is characteristically cryptic:

> For bothe I hadde thyng which that I nolde,
> And ek I nadde that thyng that I wolde.
>
> [PF 90–1

The remark can be read as implying the kind of failure in love
which the narrator of *The Boke of the Duchesse* admits with the
same obliqueness. Apart from the comment made by Africanus,
'For thow of love hast lost thy tast, I gesse', little supports this
reading except Chaucer's fondness for making his dreamer a
comically incapable or unlucky figure. The derivation of the
remark from *Boece* is not helpful, for Boethius is writing of the

anxieties which beset those who enjoy 'haboundances of
rychesses';[1] a subject of no relevance to *The Parlement*. The
dreamer's comment is perhaps best understood as it stands, as
indicating his vague sense of dissatisfaction with his personal
state of being, and the motive of his quest for 'a certeyn thing'.
Something has gone wrong which cannot be put right until the
dreamer understands the nature of the private problem confronting him, which may be clarified by the dream which is
about to relieve the 'busy hevynesse' of his contemplations. The
dream seems to provide some enlightenment through figures
which embody and enact the divided awareness that troubles
him, though it does not reveal how this conflict of interests
should be settled. That problem still remains when the dreamer
returns to his reading at the end of the poem, divided between
alternatives which seem irreconcilable.

The place of the *Somnium Scipionis* in this uneasy conflict is not
easily determined. There is no direct parallel between the events
of Scipio's story and those of the dream which follows, but a
marked contrast of attitude and purpose. Africanus' advice to
Scipio to be mindful of his immortal spirit, despising worldly
pleasures and directing his thoughts towards life hereafter,
goes unacknowledged in the garden to which Chaucer's jovial
Africanus directs his dreamer. Neither Venus nor the goddess
Nature encourages her followers to shun the delights of earthly
life, and the imaginative energy of the poem is very positively
directed towards the beauty and fascinating diversity of the
material world. In this respect the *Somnium* seems something of
a red herring, with no bearing on the vital interests of Chaucer's
poem; but it may embody an ideal in which the dreamer recognises the form of purposes which he cannot achieve in his own
life. This would explain why, despite his initial enthusiasm, his
reading leaves him not elated but depressed by the consciousness of some private frustration. What attracts him in the *Somnium*, until he is made to feel the unresolved conflict in himself,
is the prospect of reconciling an age-old alienation, which
Africanus twice describes to his grandson. The first concerns the

[1] *Boece*, iii. pr. 3. 33–6.

completion of the so-called platonic year, when all the stars will
have completed a cycle which brings them back to their starting-
points:

> Thanne tolde he hym, in certeyn yeres space
> That every sterre shulde come into his place
> Ther it was first, and al shulde out of mynde
> That in this world is don of al mankynde.

[PF 67–70

Chaucer's rendering of this passage misrepresents his original.
Africanus is not in fact speaking of the future in the *Somnium*, but
using the idea of the platonic year to make Scipio realise the
relative insignificance of the personal fame he is soon to acquire.
Chaucer makes the allusion prophetic, adding a reference to the
obliterating of all human achievement, which he did not find in
the *Somnium*, and making it appear that this event would come
at the end of a vast astronomical cycle, when the stars again
stood as at the Creation. The effect, and presumably the purpose
of this change of sense, is to suggest a return to final harmony
and perfection after ages of wandering from established order.
In this amended form the passage corresponds in idea with
Africanus' account of the eventual pardoning of those who have
followed their appetites, who

> Shul whirle aboute th'erthe alwey in peyne,
> Tyl many a world be passed, out of drede,
> And than, foryeven al hir wikked dede,
> Than shul they come into this blysful place.

[PF 80–3

This gathering-together of the virtuous and the damned in the
same sphere of heaven represents the kind of uniting and inte-
grating of opposites which the dreamer's experience repeatedly
fails to provide. Where there is a prospect of harmonious pair-
ing, it is checked by the formel's decision to postpone her choice;
and although there remains a hope of union in the future, the
poem ends without any such definite assurance as the *Somnium*
provides.

The explicit link between the *Somnium* and the narrator's own

vision is supplied by the figure of Africanus, which the sleeper's
mind takes over by the associative process which characterises
the *insomnium*. The new Africanus is a guide very little resembl-
ing the austere and awesome presence which conducts Scipio
across the heavens and discloses the moral forces acting upon
human life. Explaining that he intends to repay the dreamer for
his respectful study of 'myn olde bok totorn', Africanus seizes
him and leads the dreamer to the gate of the garden, where he
is to find the subject-matter of a poem in the varieties of earthly
love, which Scipio had been warned to shun. Like the Eagle in
The Hous of Fame, Africanus treats the dreamer with amused
condescension and no great courtesy. When the dreamer hesi-
tates before the forbidding double inscription over the gate, his
guide assures him that they have no application to him,

> Ne by non, but he Loves servaunt be: [HF 159

effectively dismissing the dreamer's right to be considered a
poet. None the less, he continues bluntly,

> although that thow be dul,
> Yit that thou canst not do, yit mayst thow se,
> For many a man that may nat stonde a pul,
> It liketh hym at the wrastlyng for to be,
> And demeth yit wher he do bet or he.
>
> [PF 162–6

The analogy with a popular sport implies an unflattering view
of the dreamer's abilities, and suggests an acquaintance with
common life which would be surprising in Scipio's Africanus.
His function is not restricted to leading the dreamer to the
starting-point of his curious adventure. Faced by the contradictory inscriptions over the entrance to the garden, the dreamer
becomes paralysed with indecision. 'For with that oon,' he
explains, referring to the warning notice,

> encresede ay my fere,
> And with that other gan myn herte bolde;
> That oon me hette, that other dide me colde.
>
> [PF 143–5

No physical obstacle prevents him from entering, but a divided
state of mind which he cannot overcome unaided. Not by accident, the two inscriptions characterise the conflict of interests
which the dream will represent to the immobilised dreamer,
who feels himself held like a piece of metal between two mag-
nets. He is only able to move forward when Africanus pushes
him unceremoniously into the garden:

> Me hente, and shof in at the gates wide.   [PF 154

Once inside, he encounters no further check, and passes
through the garden as easily as if the scene were unrolling before him: a spectator who speaks to none of the figures whom he
observes, and who describes scenes and events without any sense
of personal involvement. After the bound of pleasure which he
feels at his first sight of the garden.

> But Lord, so I was glad and wel begoon!   [PF 171

there is no further suggestion of personal conflict. The contradictions and conflicts represented in his dream are now outside
himself, in the landscape and its wonderful inhabitants.

We recognise such a feature in the passage of description
which opens the dreamer's account of the enchantingly beautiful garden in which he now finds himself. In its setting 'upon a
ryver, in a grene mede', and in its profusion of blossoming trees
and flowers, the garden conforms with the tradition honoured
by so many medieval poets; and the animals which the dreamer
notices under the trees –

> The dredful ro, the buk, the hert and hynde,
> Squyrels, and bestes smale of gentil kynde
>> [PF 195–6

– match those which Chaucer's first dreamer sees in the forest.
But what follows, in a stanza listing the individual trees and
referring briefly to their practical uses as timber, has no place in
the traditions of dream-poetry, and comes from a source well
outside the interests of courtly love:

The byldere ok, and ek the hardy asshe;
The piler elm, the cofre unto carayne;
The boxtre pipere; holm to whippes lashe;
The saylynge fyr; the cipresse, deth to playne;
The shetere ew; the asp for shaftes pleyne;
The olyve of pes, and eke the dronke vyne;
The victor palm; the laurer to devyne.

[PF 176–82

After a single introductory stanza describing the unearthly
beauty of the garden, whose trees bear leaves 'that ay shal laste',
the dreamer has suddenly shifted to a realistic appraisal of their
usefulness in the world of waking activity. Where the narrator
in *The Boke of the Duchesse* had admired the trees for their
astonishing size and dense foliage, which only a dream-forest
could produce, those standing in the garden are catalogued
according to their practical value to society, where men build
houses and ships, drive carts and shoot arrows. The references
to these activities dislodge attention from the dream-world whose
occupants abandon themselves to leisure and inertia, bringing
to mind the manual labour and the circumstances of everyday
life. Their implications seem to be strongly at variance with
Chaucer's purpose in describing the more fanciful features of
the garden, in particular its freedom from the irksome conditions of mortality:

No man may there waxe sek ne old.   [PF 207

This idea is imaginatively incompatible with the allusion to
coffin-making and 'carayne', or corpses, in the catalogue of
trees. The incompatibility can be seen as the unintended consequence of combining material from different sources, Boccaccio
and Joseph of Exeter, in the same narrative sequence. But as the
three associations of trees which most graphically suggest common life – 'the coffre unto carayne', 'holm to whippes lashe',
and 'the aspe for shaftes pleyne' – are original to Chaucer, it
would seem that he did not lift ideas from Joseph without
participating as a poet in his theme. While he is imaginatively

content to follow Boccaccio through a fantasy-world of perpetual summer which excludes all the discomforts of everyday
existence, Chaucer's mind retains an awareness of reality which
refuses to be entirely silent. Although apparently delighted by
the idealised artificiality of the garden, he can be excited by
another writer's allusions to the great variety of natural creation, and break away from his first topic to declare his admira-
tion for the power which makes reality more fascinating than
the world of the dreamer. Chaucer's purposes in *The Parlement*
seem to be determined by this polarity. Unlike other medieval
poets working within the tradition of dream-poetry, he was
evidently unable to sink himself uncritically in the fantasmal
remoteness of the dreamer's experience, or to detach himself
imaginatively from the world of fact whose characteristic figures
tend towards the comic.

For the moment, however, the dreamer is absorbed in the
serene and entrancingly beautiful world to which Africanus has
brought him – a journey which in most love-visions the narrator
is able to make unassisted. The garden resounds with angelic
birdsong, and the dream offers no hint of the very unharmonious
bird-noises which set the dreamer's teeth on edge later, when the
creatures 'of gentil kynde' are outnumbered by others of baser
rank, whose behaviour is not at all unearthly. Now, as he moves
through the garden, delighted by the music of stringed instru-
ments playing 'in acord' and by the scent of herbs and spices, he
begins to see Africanus' promise fulfilled. A succession of legendary and mythological figures, representing aspects of romantic
love, are disposed about the sunlit enclosure, to be studied by
the dreamer with eager interest. Not all of them are unequi-
vocally charming. Despite an idyllic setting 'under a tre,
besyde a welle', the first group of figures tacitly indicates the
painful injuries that love may inflict; for there Cupid displays
his destructive potentiality by forging and filing arrowheads to
which his daughter gives the cruel finishing touches,

Some for to sle, and some to wounde and kerve.
[PF 217

In another happy setting under an oak-tree the dreamer recognises two of the more winning aspects of love, Delyt standing with Gentilesse; but flanking another group of appealing attributes – Plesaunce, Aray, Lust and Curteysie – he notices one more silent warning of the hurtful influences to which lovers are exposed:

> the Craft that can and hath the myght
> To don by force a wyght to don folye
>
> [PF 220–1

The women who dance about the temple of Venus, 'in kertels, al dischevele', enliven an almost motionless scene by suggesting the carefree joyousness of those who abandon themselves to love; but the contrasting figure of Pacience, sitting fixedly outside the temple

> With face pale, upon an hil of sonde;   [PF 243

reminds the dreamer again of the pain which the lover may endure, when faithful service brings no reward. The followers of Byheste and Art, who swarm about and inside the temple, represent other aspects of the disappointment which may await the lover, in unfulfilled promises and guileful inducements.

Venus herself, dimly seen in the warm darkness of her temple, combines the attraction and the threat which love offers its servants. The moans of her victims which echo through the building, in 'sykes hoote as fyr', suggest the tragic force of sexual desire which has its centre in her recumbent nakedness. 'Ful noble and hautayn', the goddess lies on a golden bed, only partly covered by a flimsy costume, her unbound hair caught up by a single thread of gold, waiting for night to fall.[1] Sitting with her as attendants, Bacchus and Ceres suggest the pleasure of feasting, and also the tipsiness which, as the Wife of Bath knows, readily leads to sexual indulgence. They are accompanied by two mortal figures, kneeling in supplication as they beg Venus to help them: another indication of the distress which love

---

[1] Although the garden enjoys perpetual day [line 209], the associations of Venus with night oblige Chaucer to be inconsistent.

causes. Further from the goddess, but occupying a place of honour in the temple, Priapus is accorded by worshippers who crown him with garlands of fresh flowers; evidently paying reverence to the shameless sexuality revealed by his attempt to ravish the nymph Lotis. The dreamer maintains his objective detachment, not protesting at their honouring of priapism; though when he comments on the broken bows of the young women who abandoned Diana's service, speaking of

> maydenes swiche as gonne here tymes waste [PF 283

he seems to accept the outlook of Venus' followers. This impression is not maintained in his description of the paintings covering the walls of the temple, which commemorate some of the most famous lovers of legend and history:

> Semyramis, Candace and Hercules,
> Biblis, Dido, Thisbe and Piramus,
> Tristram, Isaude, Paris, and Achilles,
> Eleyne, Cleopatre, and Troylus,
> Silla, and ek the moder of Romulus:
> Alle these were peynted on that other syde,
> And al here love, and in what plyt they dyde.
>
> [PF 288–94

The list includes figures notorious for crimes of incest and adultery, and has a common element in the desperation which drove many of these lovers to death by suicide or through inconsolable grief. As in the other two dream-poems, what Chaucer here describes as a picture belongs primarily to literary tradition, and the conspicuous place given to these painted figures in the temple represents the respectful treatment of romantic suicide in courtly writing of the time. The dreamer, again a seemingly impartial spectator, does not resist this valuation of self-destructive frenzy; though earlier, speaking of the impulse which can 'force a wyght to don folye', he appears to show approval of emotional moderation and good sense. His closing comment on the paintings,

> al here love, and in what plyt they dyde [PF 294

is left to make its point tacitly by associating romantic love with agonising forms of death.

Significantly, the description of the garden ends with this reference to death. Although the dreamer has shown a keen appreciation of the natural beauty of the garden, declaring that it gave him

> joye more a thousandfold
> Than man can telle;   [PF 208–9

its personifications of love suggest both pleasure and pain, and admit various forms of 'grevaunce' not otherwise found in the garden. Unlike its evergreen trees, and its ignorance of sickness and old age, the closed world of Venus presents a threat of starving winter,

> Ther nevere tre shal fruyt ne leves bere.   [PF 137

This muted association of Venus with sterility and death may prompt us to recognise how many of the figures in the garden are motionless and inert, as though frozen into symbolic attitudes which cannot be varied. To the extent that Chaucer is following tradition this may seem natural enough. The allegorical figures in *The Parlement* are a conventional equivalent of the many 'riche portraitures' studied by the dreamer in the *Roman de la Rose*, and duplicated in many later dream-poems, including Chaucer's. But comparison with the dreamer's account of the Virgilian mural in *The Hous of Fame*, which is the parallel episode of that poem, shows Chaucer giving lively impulse and animation to painted images. The goddess who appears to Aeneas in the guise of a huntress,

> With wynd blowynge upon hir tresse;   [HF 230

breaks out of fixity into the freshness of outdoors, much as the dreamer in *The Boke of the Duchesse* leaps from his painted bedchamber into the activity of the chase. The immobility of the legendary figures seen by the dreamer in *The Parlement of Foules*, and the impression of a closed atmosphere which is particularly

strong inside the temple, with its 'thousand savours sote', are
felt partly in the dreamer's relief as he moves from the emotionally charged environment of Venus and her attendants to the
grassy clearing where Nature has called her annual parliament.
His comment,

> Forth welk I tho myselven to solace   [PF 297

is strikingly unlike the response of the previous Chaucerian
dreamer, who leaves another temple of Venus dazed by the
craftsmanship of its architect and painter. The figures in the
garden, set in unvarying attitudes, have the interest only of
studied artifice, and while they may interest the dreamer he
gives no sign of being excited by them. It is only when he
exchanges this fixed and timeless world for the natural simpli-
city of the birds' gathering-place that he begins to become
emotionally involved in the scene. His description of the goddess who is to preside over the parliament represents a radical
change of mood as well as of subject-matter:

> And in a launde, upon an hil of floures,
> Was set this noble goddesse Nature.
> Of braunches were here halles and here boures,
> Iwrought after here cast and here mesure.
>
> [PF 302-5

Both the setting and the materials of this informal building contrast strongly with the artificiality of the temple which the
dreamer has just left, made of brass and supported by 'pilers
greete of jasper longe'. As in *The Hous of Fame*, the dreamer
moves from a typical dream-palace occupied by imposing but
motionless legendary figures to a building almost too casually
constructed to be considered a work of architecture. Like the
house of interwoven twigs in the previous poem, this meeting-
hall of branches designed by Nature herself bears no relation to
human craftsmanship, whose ingenuity might be incapable of
devising a building large enough to house the mass of creatures
among whom, once again, the dreamer barely finds room to
stand:

erthe, and eyr, and tre, and every lake
So ful was, that unethe was there space
For me to stonde, so ful was al the place.   [PF 313-15

Despite the noise and struggling confusion of so great a crowd, the goddess imposes a rudimentary form of order upon the birds by arranging them according to rank in the natural hierarchy, giving eagles and other birds of prey pride of place and water-fowl the lowest position, befitting their association with a lower element. Although logical, this respect for order is evidently not shared by the dreamer, for when he comes to list the different kinds of bird gathered for the ceremony he follows an arbitrary plan. Like the narrator of *The General Prologue*, who apologises for failing to 'set folk in hir degree', he begins with the most socially distinguished members of the gathering, but quickly loses all sense of gradation. After presenting the birds of prey as a group, he mentions next the dove, the swan and the owl, and continues in random order as though enthusing over the diversity of natural kinds.

This impulse seems to direct the catalogue of trees and their practical uses earlier in the poem. The much longer list, taking up five stanzas and touching upon thirty-six different kinds of bird, provides a still more impressive tribute to the inventiveness of nature. Although some of the qualities attributed to individual birds are merely fabulous, like the eagle's ability to stare into the sun, the mixture of mythical and factual itself helps to diversify the dreamer's excited survey. The greater part of his catalogue is taken up with birds of the English countryside, described in epithets or brief connotations which suggest the dreamer's affectionate familiarity with their habits and habitat:

The crane, the geaunt, with his trompes soun;
The thef, the chough, and ek the janglynge pye;
The skornynge jay; the eles fo, heroun;
The false lapwynge, ful of trecherye;
The stare, that the conseyl can bewrye;
The tame ruddok, and the coward kyte;
The kok, that orloge is of thorpes lyte.

[PF 344-50

These are not the incredible creatures of a dream, but a small part of created life whose endless variations of form and kind are both more astonishing and – because actual – more satisfying than the figures of fantasy. Although nominally asleep, the dreamer has surfaced into everyday life where magpies chatter in the woods, and the village cock wakes a labouring community to another day. With this renewed awareness of reality the poem turns away from the fanciful conditions of the garden and acknowledges winter, old age and death.

> The jelous swan, ayens his deth that syngeth;
> The oule ek, that of deth the bode bryngeth;
>
> [PF 342–3

are two birds which should have no place inside the garden. The list ends by mentioning three more birds whose natures suggest the sadness and discomfort of the human winter:

> the crowe with vois of care;
> The throstil old; the frosty feldefare.   [PF 363–4

As in the catalogue of trees, the incompatibility of these birds with the timeless garden is not explained by supposing that Chaucer overlooked the garden's immunity to change and decay. His imagination is engaged simultaneously by two distinct subjects, both of which excite him. The artifice of the garden makes its appeal by evoking a picture of a ravishingly beautiful world, liberated from the susceptibility to time, disease and death which disfigures man's actual existence. But despite these limitations, or indeed because of them, the actual world makes its own powerful appeal through the much greater diversity of experience which it provides. Perpetual summer could become tedious, while the cycle of seasonal change constantly varies the interest of the natural world. Life restricted by timelessness to a single state of development lacks a vital quality which is only found when old age and death are accepted as part of its process. Chaucer's catalogue of birds, which represents not only the astonishing range of kinds within a single species but also the vast variety of their individual characters, declares a poet's enthusiasm for the world of natural creation. In the conflict of interests between actual and ideal, the homely thrush and the wintry fieldfare are exerting a claim upon Chaucer's imaginative attention which seem likely to displace his interest in courtly figures.

Nature herself, however, does not reserve her favours for the birds which live by impulse, and who choose their mates with concern for the needs of 'engendrure'. The bird she holds on her hand and occasionally kisses belongs to the highest level of the social hierarchy, and is also the most attractive of her creatures:

> A formel egle, of shap the gentilleste
> That evere she among hire werkes fond,
> The most benygne and the goodlieste;
> In hire was everi vertu at his reste.   [PF 373-6

Her respect for social rank and its accompanying qualities is shown again when the goddess announces her purpose in the speech which opens the parliament. In accordance with custom the birds have assembled on St Valentine's Day to choose their mates, in an order determined by social status and beginning with whichever bird 'most is worthi'. As though to remove any doubt she names the tercel eagle as superior to them all, enumerating the qualities that accompany social distinction and admitting her special pride in him:

> The foul royal, above yow in degre,
> The wyse and worthi, secre, trewe as stel,
> Which I have formed, as ye may wel se,
> In every part as it best liketh me.   [PF 394-7

We might think Nature a snob, but as 'vicaire of the almyghty Lord' the goddess has a particular interest in maintaining due order and precedence, which form part of the universal design entrusted to her. The superiority of the courtly birds is not simply an attribute of social rank; rather, it comes about through the unusual beauty or intelligence naturally bestowed on them. Within the context of love the particular qualities of the tercel eagle, and especially his discretion and constancy, must arouse heightened respect, for these are characteristics required of the courtly lover, and represent the highest expression of the impulse which has brought all the birds together. How completely the royal tercel has sublimated the crude energies of sex into a gentle and gracious appeal for consideration appears as soon as he begins to address the formel. Describing her as 'my soverayn lady, and not my fere' or mate, he offers his faithful and unquestioning service, and makes the traditional request for pity and condescension:

> Besekynge hire of merci and of grace,
> As she that is my lady sovereyne;
> Or let me deye present in this place:
> For certes, longe may I nat lyve in payne,
> For in myn herte is korven every veyne.
> Havynge reward only to my trouthe,
> My deere herte, have on my wo som routhe.
>
> [PF 421-7]

Although largely dictated by convention, his appeal commits the lover irrevocably to his choice. Any return the lady gives will be impelled not by sexual attraction but by respect for the lover's 'trouthe' or pledged fidelity, and this pledge will prevent him from transferring his affections to another mistress if this affair does not prosper. The criticisms later brought against *fine amour* by the lower birds help to show how the courtly sublimation of the sexual drive ends by defeating the natural purpose of this impulse. The lover whose appeals are resisted is condemned to a lifetime of celibacy, and to futile persistence in a course where constancy must eventually mock itself.

Watched by the dreamer, two other suitors repeat the substance of the royal tercel's protestations and commit themselves to the same unswerving service of the lady, staking their lives upon their fidelity; though with considerable difference of expression. The second tercel, 'of lower kynde', answers his rival with a boastful speech claiming to have loved and served the formel eagle no less ardently, and brazenly asserts his right to the 'gerdonynge' which should reward such constancy. The demands condemns the speaker by its impudence, but he is already betrayed by his uncouth and self-assertive language.

'That shal nat be!' he blurts out defiantly, without troubling to acknowledge the formel's presence,

> 'I love hire bet than ye don, by seint John,
> Or at the leste I love hire as wel as ye,
> And lenger have served hire in my degre.'
>
> [PF 451-3

Matching the first speaker point by point, he too offers his life as pledge of his true service, but in language whose aggressive energy is incongruously out of keeping with the sense of his declaration:

> 'I dar ek seyn, if she me fynde fals,
> Unkynde, janglere, or rebel any wyse,
> Or jelous, do me hangen by the hals!'   [PF 456-8

This reference to hanging, like the oath earlier in his speech, give a foretaste of the comic purpose which is soon to dominate the poem. The dream is again wearing thin, and beginning to admit glimpses of common life. The speech of the first tercel does not suggest this, for the courteous idea which he expresses is as appropriately dreamlike as the perfect beauty of the formel to whom he dedicates himself. But as the speeches edge closer to colloquial informality the dream becomes more and more of a joke, whose characters' fantasmal quality is balanced against unmistakable elements of waking reality.

This impression is strengthened by the third tercel, who although more respectfully restrained than the previous speaker, leaps into credible being with an expansive appeal to good sense which concludes with an almost perfunctory declaration of his hopeless love. 'Now sires, ye seen the lytel leyser heere', he begins, immediately reaching out for an agreeable understanding with his audience,

> 'For every foul cryeth out to ben ago
> Forth with his make, or with his lady deere;
> And ek Nature hireself ne wol not heere,
> For taryinge here, not half that I wolde seye,
> And but I speke, I mot for sorwe deye.'
>
> [PF 465-9

Since public interest forbids any extravagant display of feeling –
everyone is anxious to leave as soon as possible – the speaker
promises to confine himself to a few well-chosen words. He does
not intend to boast of his long service, for what counts is not
mere duration but the intensity of the lover's feelings; and his
unrequited passion may kill him on the spot, where another
suitor may languish 'twenty winter' without ill effects. This
workaday phrase and the unashamedly realistic tone of his
argument help to place the speech in the world of common
affairs, whose inhabitants Chaucer had obviously been studying
with the discernment that would find fullest expression in *The
General Prologue*. The dreamer seems not to recognise how much
the three suitors differ in temperament and manner, for he is
much moved by the whole scene, and at the end of their
speeches he remarks that in all his life

> syn that day I was born,
> So gentil ple in love or other thyng
> Ne herde nevere no man me beforn.   [PF 484–6

The lower birds do not share his feelings. Most of the day has
already been spent in the 'cursede pletynge' of the courtly
suitors, and they are now impatient to seize their mates and be
away, without wasting further time over fruitless arguments:

> 'How sholde a juge eyther parti leve
> For ye or nay, withouten any preve?'   [PF 496–7

The dreamer's approving comment on the 'gentil ple' of the
courtly birds helps to make such protests seem ill-mannered and
unreasonable. That is probably the immediate function of the
remark, which tries to suppress the reader's awareness of the
defiant and self-assertive tone of the two later speakers. The outburst of cawing and cackling which supports the lower birds'
protest obscures the good sense of their objection that it is impossible to judge between the unsupported claims made by the
three suitors. Almost deafened by the hubbub, the dreamer is
also denied any quiet opportunity for reflecting that since only
one of them can be accepted, at least two of the formel's devoted
servants have just condemned themselves to a permanently un-

productive existence. The reader too is distracted from a more
critical judgement of courtly standards by the sheer vulgarity of
their opponents, whose mindless squawking grates in the ear:

> The goos, the cokkow, and the doke also
> So cryede, 'Kek kek! kokkow! quek quek!' hye,
> That thourgh myne eres the noyse wente tho.
> The goos seyde, 'Al this nys not worth a flye!'
>
> [PF 498–501

Chaucer is evidently employing the same device as he uses to
persuade his reader in *The Boke of the Duchesse* that his narrator is
a comically misguided judge of facts and values, whose deprecia-
tion of courtly standards does not call for any answer. This
would not imply that Chaucer secretly supports the lower birds
in their scorn for the elaborate code of *fine amour* and the
romantic agony it promotes, and that he declares himself
obliquely through the clownish goose and duck. *The Parlement*
would be a much easier poem to understand if Chaucer's position were so simple and unambiguous. That position is complicated by the special affection shown by Nature towards the
noble birds who, although honouring St Valentine's Day,
remain without mates at the end of the long debate. The male
eagles are not entirely to blame for their continued bachelor-
dom; but they accept a system which does not have 'engendrure' as its purpose, and which accepts frustration and the
waste of sexual potential as a consequence of its attitude towards
love. A modern reader may think the formel eagle much more
at fault in deciding to remain unmarried for another year, for
this means that both she and her three suitors will play no part
in the creative scheme during that time. Whether maiden
modesty prompts her decision or the kind of physical aversion
from marriage admitted by Emily in *The Knight's Tale*,[1] the
goddess receives her appeal sympathetically, and then dismisses
the birds as though to forestall any protest, telling the suitors:

[1] 'Chaste goddesse, wel wostow that I/Desire to ben a mayden al my
lyf . . . And for to walken in the wodes wilde,/And noght to ben a wyf and
be with childe.' – *CT* I.2304–5, 2309–10.

Beth of goode herte, and serveth alle thre.
A yer is nat so longe to endure,
And ech of yow peyne him in his degre
For to do wel.

[PF 660–63

The reminder that a year will soon pass cannot be a true con-
solation for all three tercels, since two of them must be finally
disappointed. If the poem is to be read as a criticism of the code
which encourages this laming of creative purpose, then Chaucer's
goddess of Nature must be seen as the enemy of her own generative purpose. Obviously such a reading will not do.

It might be a simpler to argue that by exposing the ideals of
fine amour to the uncouth commentary of the lower birds,
Chaucer was proving it a code of manners too refined to be
understood by the insensitive. But this would not be a very
plausible way of recommending *fine amour*; and moreover, some
of the criticisms made by the lower birds are not easily shrugged
off. It could, however, be a means of testing the value of a code
designed to operate within the closed circle of courtly life – or,
more probably, of courtly literature – by taking it outside its
protected environment, where its typical attitudes have to justify
themselves against a background of everyday life and opinions.
Whether or not this was Chaucer's intention, the poem has this
effect. The parliament first provides a platform for the courtly
birds to declare the principles of their highly artificial society,
and then allows a variety of commonsense opinions about love
and sexual attraction to be expressed by the other birds, most of
which are predictably unromantic and practical. This is certainly true of the goose, who opens the debate with a down-to-
earth judgement which cuts across the suitors' fine sentiments
with devastating bluntness:

I seye I rede hym, though he were my brother,
But she wol love hym, lat hym love another!

[PF 566–7

This suggestion produces an indignant response from the
sparrowhawk, who as a bird of prey assumes the right to defend

the standards of courtly behaviour, though with a roughness of manner which betrays his own lack of breeding:

> Lo, swich it is to have a tonge loos!
> Now parde, fol! yit were it bet for the
> Han holde thy pes than shewed thy nycete.
>
> [PF 570–2

Comparison with the angry outbursts of some of the more churlish of the Canterbury pilgrims suggests that the sparrowhawk is using the vocabulary and idiomatic forms of popular speech, which Chaucer now handles with fluency and assurance: a power which has its part in determining the design of the poem. The turtle-dove speaks next, and reveals a temperament as unlike the sparrowhawk's as his attitude to love, which adapts a central precept of *fine amour* to sentimental taste:

> 'Nay, God forbede a lovere shulde chaunge!'
> The turtle seyd, and wex for shame al red,
> 'Though that his lady everemore be straunge,
> Yit lat hym serve hire ever, til he be ded.'
>
> [PF 582–5

This blushing extremism puts the courtly case rather too simply for the speaker to be accepted as its authentic spokesman: like the Prioress whom he brings to mind, the turtle-dove wishes to claim a kinship with the courtly world which has no basis in his social status. The duck dismisses his argument with a derisive compliment:

> 'Wel bourded,' quod the doke, 'by myn hat!'
> That men shulde loven alwey causeles,
> Who can a resoun fynde or wit in that?
> Daunseth he murye that is myrtheles?'
>
> [PF 589–92

The proverbial remark which completes his comment, 'There been mo sterres, God wot, than a payre!' adds the force of popular wisdom to this brusque appeal to commonsense. Here again the cogency of the speaker's criticism is obscured by an impression of self-opinionated ignorance, which the duck confirms by his emphatic, 'Ye, quek!' as he winds up his speech. But when his question is considered apart from the speaker's over-vigorous terms, and courtly ideals are brought face to face with his challenge,

'Who can a resoun fynde or wit in that?'   [PF 591

we must recognise that the romantic idealist has a case to answer. The obvious purpose of sexual attraction is 'engendrure' or natural increase, and the lover who persists in wooing despite the lady's repeated rejection of his offered service, or who remains constant to a dead mistress, is gratifying a self-indulgent whim where he should be promoting the creative purpose of Nature. The courtly lover might argue that human behaviour is not, or should not be, determined simply by natural impulse, and that noble character is revealed in a refusal to follow instinctive promptings blindly. More to the point in this poem, he could point out that the goddess herself feels a special affection for the formel eagle, preferring her to any of the lower-class birds who do her will by promptly choosing their mates; and that when she recommends the royal tercel,

As for the gentilleste and most worthi,
Which I have wrought so wel to my plesaunce,
[PF 634-5

she admits a personal interest in – and even a responsibility for – the courtly nature of this noble suitor. It may be right to assume that although she calls the birds into assembly with the purpose of their mating, this is not her only concern; and that as Nature she has a lively interest in the diversity of her creatures. There is not much need to speculate about the purposes of one of Chaucer's characters when the poem itself proves his imaginative excitement at the unlimited variety of natural life. The catalogue of trees included in a thoroughly conventional description of the garden, and the much fuller list of birds which extends the poet's terms of reference still further, represent an outburst of pleasure at the range of natural creation. If the goddess does not share this pleasure, Chaucer certainly feels it himself; for *The Parlement* is progressively impelled by a recognition that the natural world contains more delightful and astonishing creatures than are stored in the temples of art. The multitude of voices and personalities which break into activity during the birds' debate, giving the poem a vitality lacking in the description of the garden, suggest how completely Chaucer has embraced the principle of diversity over which Nature sits in authority.

Three more opinions bring the debate to the point where the goddess must exert that authority to wind up the argument. The duck's downright judgement provokes an indignant retort from one of the tercels, who forgets his breeding in the excitement of hearing his social code ridiculed:

> 'Now fy, cherl!' quod the gentil tercelet,
> 'Out of the donghil cam that word ful right! . . .
> Thy kynde is of so lowe a wrechednesse
> That what love is, thow canst nat seen ne gesse.'
>
> [PF 596–602

No doubt many other birds would echo his opinion, for the debate has revealed a disagreement about the nature of love much wider than the simple disparity between courtly and plebian attitudes. The variety of temperamental outlook is further extended as a new voice, cynically indifferent towards the discomfort of others, breaks in with the cuckoo's complacently selfish comment:

> 'So I,' quod he, 'may have myn make in pes,
> I reche nat how longe that ye stryve.
> Lat eche of hem ben soleyn al here lyve!'
>
> [PF 605–7

This scornful opinion proves too much for the merlin's self-restraint, and he bursts out against the cuckoo's nature and habits in a speech which outrages all sense of politeness:

> 'Thow mortherere of the heysoge on the braunche
> That brought the forth: thou rewtheles glotoun!
> Lyve thow soleyn, wermis corupcioun!'
>
> [PF 612–14

At this point Nature intervenes and winds up the debate. She
has now heard all their arguments, she tells the birds, and it
must be clear to them all that they are as far from agreement as
ever. Since an open debate has failed to reach a solution, she
decides to leave the formel eagle to make her own decision;
allowing her to make free choice of her suitors without respecting any other consideration than her own feelings. This freedom
of choice is in fact rather less open than Nature implies, since the
goddess remarks that if she were Reason her preference would be
for the royal tercel: a hint difficult for the formel to ignore, even
if reason is not the surest guide in affairs of the heart. But by
intervening in a debate that was rapidly degenerating into an
unparliamentary brawl, Nature seems about to resolve its contradictory arguments and prejudices into a single point of view;
and her bold assertion of authority,

> 'Thus juge I, Nature, for I may not lye!'   [PF 629

encourages the reader to suppose that the problem which the
birds have been quarrelling over is about to be settled.

The formel eagle's decision not to take a mate disappoints
this expectation. In the respect that her aversion to marriage
represents one more attitude to love, her slighting of Venus and
Cupid has a logical place in the survey which the poem carries
out; and since Nature accepts her decision it appears that the
formel is not thwarting her purposes. Possibly Nature's hand is
forced, for she promises in advance to grant the formel's request,
and cannot retract her pledged word when she learns that the
formel wishes to remain unmarried. But it would be misleading
to suggest that Nature is exclusively concerned with procreation
and the maintenance of created life, as Boethius might encourage his readers to suppose.[1] She is also the power responsible
for the order and balance of earthly life, who

> hot, cold, hevy, lyght, moyst and drye
> Hath knyt by evene noumbres of acord,   [PF 380–1

---

[1] 'Nature desireth and requireth alwey . . . the work of generacioun, by
which generacioun only duelleth and is susteyned the long durablete of
mortel thingis' – *Boece* III. pr. 11, 171–5.

and it is her creative energy and inventiveness which has produced the astonishing diversity of living creatures which the
poet describes before the birds begin their parliament. Nature
has not one purpose but many, and gives each living kind its
inclination and individuality, the courtly no less than the common. Chaucer makes the goddess respectful of the temperamental differences which separate the birds, even when this
liberality prevents her from imposing a conclusion upon the
debate which would have given the poem a definite outcome.
When it appears that the argument has reached a final impasse,
the goddess wastes no further time in discussion but dissolves the
assembly without more ado:

> Quod tho Nature, 'Heere is no more to seye.
> Thanne wolde I that these foulis were aweye,
> Eche with his make, for taryinge lengere heere!"   [PF 655-7

Her parting advice to the tercels offers no criticism of the code
which all three profess to follow. 'Beth of goode herte, and
serveth alle thre' acknowledges that the principles of *fine amour*
fall within Nature's sphere of interest, as a directing impulse
proper to those to whom she has given courtly nature and
instincts. Each of the three suitors is to 'peyne hym in his degre'
to render true service to the formel throughout the coming year,
using this interval for self-improvement within the code, while
the formel remains outside the field of courtly love in a position
whose neutrality is guaranteed by Nature.

While the courtly birds are immobilised by a year's delay, the
rest of the parliament dissolves in a spirit of exuberant happiness
which finds lyrical outlet in a roundel celebrating the end of
winter, with its 'longe nyghtes blake', and welcoming the
approach of summer's warmth and softness. As they disperse,
their excited shouting wakes the dreamer; and he at once
returns to his interrupted search in 'othere bokys', as though
too much preoccupied with his unfinished quest to recognise
any significance for himself in the events of his dream. Where the
dreamer of *The Boke of the Duchesse* immediately sets to work
upon a poem describing his strange experience, his counterpart

in *The Parlement* ignores the 'mater of to wryte' presented to him by Africanus, and goes back to his books as though for enlightenment which the dream has failed to provide. His seeming indifference to what he has seen is another strange feature of the poem's conclusion: a state of emotional unresponsiveness at odds with the jubilant feelings of the common birds, though perhaps not unlike the attitude of the tercels, who are left to wear out another year in unrewarded service. To him as to them the parliament has brought only encouragement to contain himself patiently until his problem can find positive resolution at some later date.

But although the dreamer returns to waking consciousness without the 'certeyn thyng' which he hoped to learn, the dream obviously holds a significance for the poet despite its unresolved ending. What it represents of Chaucer's own imaginative position can be grasped initially in the contrast between the two parts of the dream; one taken over from Boccaccio and dealing respectfully with the traditional love-vision, the other original to Chaucer and full of unexpected developments. Not the least of those is the debate which allows representatives of plebeian life to criticise *fine amour* from the standpoint of everyday judgement, and in language which brings the idiom of the market-place into abrasive contact with courtly refinement. The contrast between the two sections of the dream is itself a vital condition of the great assembly, where an instinctive and a highly sophisticated code of manners meet in conflict. As the dreamer passes from the charming *tableaux vivants* of the garden to the freshness and spontaneity of the open-air parliament, he indicates the course of imaginative development which has carried Chaucer to this point of poetic growth. Like the dreamer, Chaucer has moved from a limited, formalised and predictable field of experience into a bigger landscape offering a much wider range of figures and happenings, where extremes of outlook meet. In both previous dream-poems Chaucer shows an inclination to break away from courtly tradition by introducing a comic element into an habitually sober form of writing. In *The Parlement* this comic impulse becomes so assertive that only the authority of

Nature can repress its boisterous energy, which threatens to discredit *fine amour* and to dominate the discussion by its realistic and forceful opinions. As no compromise can be found between the attitudes of the courtly birds and their plebeian critics, so no other means of combining the imaginative interests which they represent offers itself to Chaucer than the inconclusive debate which allows both to find expression. Evidently he was not ready to discard the poetic tradition which had provided the basis and motivation of his early work. Indeed, he never did reject it completely, for even as late and uncourtly a poem as *The Miller's Tale* borrows ideas and forms of speech from *fine amour* to spice its comic situations. Even when he is exploiting the comic potentialities of the popular *fabliau* Chaucer remains in feeling and craftsmanship a courtly poet, working well outside its limited interests and with a far richer vocabulary, but with the intelligence and critical insight which reading and a cosmopolitan experience have sharpened to a cutting edge.

Perhaps we come nearest to understanding *The Parlement of Foules* by looking forward from this midpoint of Chaucer's career to its final accomplishment in *The Canterbury Tales*. In the last of the three dream-poems the tension between romantic ideal and reality is more obvious than before, and the pressures of actuality more insistent. There are few moments in *The Hous of Fame* where the poem evokes a sense of direct contact with common life, though the scraps of dialogue tossed from mouth to mouth by the rumour-mongers give the reader, as well as the dreamer, an impression of the everyday experience promised by the Eagle. *The Boke of the Duchesse* provides even less contact with the world outside the dream; but in *The Parlement* Chaucer takes a long imaginative stride towards a subject and a matching comic style incompatible with the traditions of the love-vision. His third dream-poem shows him encroaching upon a new theme, asserting its own idiom and assuming a new field of reference: the actuality of life outside the circle of courtly refinement, where behaviour is impulsive and uncouth, and where human character takes as many forms as there are species of birds or trees in the natural world. Set against this rich

abundance and variety, the traditional standards of courtly
behaviour and address – the formulaic declarations, the pre-
scribed emotional responses, the worn vocabulary to which the
lover is committed – might appear lifeless and stilted. *The Boke
of the Duchesse* shows that, from the first, Chaucer's handling of
this literary convention had involved a subdued criticism of its
refusal to acknowledge the practical terms of human existence.
In the Man in Black the ideal has been allowed to blot out all
sense of the actual, the dream prolonged into a perpetual trance
whose sleeper never returns to waking consciousness. This could
not be Chaucer's way. His dreamer never becomes so absorbed
in his dream that he loses sight of the world of everyday fact –
about which he is not very well-informed – or overlooks the
artificiality and emotional extremism of the courtly code.

He certainly has no opportunity of ignoring the claims of
reality in *The Parlement of Foules*, for the birds themselves force
their plebeian tastes and attitudes upon his attention, and
declare their opinions with all the diversity of individual temperament that Chaucer had obviously studied in men. But the
dreamer's awareness of waking reality is expressed long before
the debate begins. Although affecting to know little about
human affairs at first hand, when he associates the elm with
coffins or picks out the wintry fieldfare among the assembled
birds he displays for a moment the wide-awake judgement which
unobtrusively directs the whole poem. After a confident start the
love-vision encounters difficulties which seem designed to test
the validity of the assumptions underlying its code of courtly
behaviour. The ideal standards of *fine amour* are challenged to
justify themselves against the simple unavoidable demands of
common life which, unlike the formel's decision, cannot be put
off out of delicacy or good breeding. Less obviously, the matter-
of-fact outlook of the more realistic birds is tried against a
system of values which regards their materialist arguments as
ignoble. The disparity between the two points of view is too
wide to be bridged, and although Chaucer is imaginatively
committed to both the courtly and the plebeian fields of experience, he is evidently unable to find a means of combining and

fusing both interests within the same poem. The day-long debate ends in deadlock, the formel eagle postpones her decision, and her suitors fly away to begin the year's wait that must elapse before their problem is resolved. The final implication of this undetermined outcome is that Chaucer is representing his uncertainty in the face of a challenge to his future development as a poet. The sense of actuality evoked during the birds' debate indicates the nature of his eventual achievement as a poet, but for the moment that remains a distant prospect whose form has still to be worked out. The comprehensive view of reality provided by *The Canterbury Tales* proves that the imaginative problem was not to remain unsolved.

V

CONCLUSION

THE resolution of Chaucer's problem did not involve the complete rejection of the imaginative design which he had followed in his dream-poems. Although *The Canterbury Tales* are firmly rooted in everyday reality, with a presiding figure who typifies bourgeois commonsense and worldly experience, some of the important circumstances of the early poems persist, changed but still recognisable in the central situation of the great final work. The visionary background hardens into the familiar realities of Southwark and the Canterbury road, and the fantasmal figures of the earlier encounters take on solidity and sharpness of outline, though with voices which sometimes recall the snatches of colloquial speech heard in the dreams. The narrator himself is no longer asleep during his adventure, but jostled by the crowd of aggressively individual pilgrims pressing round the story-teller of the moment, though still a reporter rather than a participant in the main event. The persistence of this condition of the dream-poems suggests that although the narrator has emerged from fantasy into the liveliness of an English April, things are continuing to happen to him much as before; and that despite being absorbed into the world of fact he remains substantially the same person as the early poems reveal.

The development of this essentially comic character is an important feature of Chaucer's early work, for it provides a clear indication of the purpose which was eventually to dominate both his outlook and his writing. In the first of the dream-poems, which is also Chaucer's first appreciable undertaking as a poet, this comic impulse is hesitant, making no attempt to declare itself in the sombre opening episodes of the story. The narrator, oppressed by sleeplessness and melancholia, is in no mood for light-hearted comments; though as he moves away from the

direct influence of Froissart and offers some cryptic remarks
about the source of his depression he shows some flickers of wry
humour, enlivened with a proverbial saying which brings him
closer to us. There is only one physician who might bring him
relief, he observes mysteriously, and immediately drops the
subject with a realistic comment:

> but that is don.
> Passe we over untill eft;
> That wil not be mote nede be left;
> Our first mater is good to kepe.   [BD 40–3

The dreamer's character begins to take shape: a man rueful over
his failure as a lover 'this eight yeer', but able to take his lack of
success philosophically, as a fact to be accepted without extravagant protest. His realistic attitude, and the homely form of his
comment, do not suggest a courtly speaker; and although the
reference to a servant who brings the narrator a romance, and
the explanation

> For me thoughte it beter play
> Than play either at ches or tables   [BD 50–1

imply an upper-class background, this impression is not firmly
registered. It is certainly not sustained by the form of the narrator's remarks after reading the tale of Alcyone and Seys, though
his emotional reactions to the story conform very closely with
the convention of aristocratic feeling. His conversational manner
shows no sense of courtly dignity or composure, but the idiomatic energy of popular speech:

> For thus moche dar I saye wel,
> I had be dolven everydel,
> And ded, ryght thurgh defaute of slep,
> Yif I ne had red and take kep
> Of this tale next before.   [BD 221–5

With this vigorously colloquial manner, Chaucer gives his
dreamer a comic potentiality which could only be realised outside the courtly conventions of the love-vision. His readiness to

K

look beyond these conventional limits of the genre is strikingly indicated in the raucous comedy of the messenger's attempts to wake Morpheus, set incongruously in a tragic tale of bereavement; though because the dreamer is apparently repeating another writer's story, he cannot be held responsible for this irreverent intrusion upon courtly feeling. But his remarks at the end of this tale, which are not open to this excuse, seem to prove that he is unable to repond appropriately to its pathos because his ignorance prevents him from realising the significance of what he has read. His first acquaintance with mythology puzzles him. 'Me thoghte wonder yf hit were so,' he admits, and concedes his previous unawareness of

> goddes that koude make
> Men to slepe, ne for to wake. [BD 235-6

This ignorance of the courtly poet's literary background, which supplies some of the essential figures of the love-vision, characterises the dreamer in each of Chaucer's three poems. Because his limited personal experience and intellectual slowness leave him unable to grasp even some of the basic principles of courtly outlook and behaviour, the dreamer is doubly mystified by his curious experience, and in his bewilderment he is confirmed as a comic figure. At this early point of *The Boke of the Duchesse* the full development of the character still lies ahead; but as the dreamer offers to reward Morpheus with a feather-bed, and amiably extends the bargain to Juno 'or som wight elles', it is already clear that his function is to be partly comic.

Not much of the immediate sequel supports this impression. As the dreamer falls asleep, to be delighted by 'so ynly swete a sweven' that perhaps not even Macrobius had a dream to rival it, his reaction conforms silently with literary tradition. That is true also of the reference to Macrobius, for although the passage displays little more knowledge of the *Somnium Scipionis* than might be gathered by hearsay, it assures us that the dreamer is not quite as ignorant of literature as his earlier remarks suggest. He continues to defer to tradition as the poem follows a predictable pattern, describing the happiness of waking to a May

morning of sunshine and birdsong, in a bedchamber[1] whose
decorative figures the dreamer at once recognises as characters
of two almost legendary works of literature,

> Of Ector and of kyng Priamus,
> Of Achilles and Lamedon,
> And eke of Medea and of Jason,   [BD 328–30

the last two later to be scorned when the dreamer dismisses
romantic love as foolishness. As he leaps from his bed to join the
departing hunt, the dreamer renews his original association with
the courtly world, making his way to the head of the cavalcade
with the confidence of social rank, and commenting on the ritual
procedure as though he were no stranger to the royal hunt. Now
nothing in the dreamer's behaviour suggests either the temperament which prefers reading to chess or backgammon or the
absurd ignoramus who bribes Morpheus with a feather bed. If
Chaucer has been experimenting with variations on the traditional dreamer, he has now returned to a more familiar literary
figure in this cultured habitué of the polite society made familiar
by the love-visions of earlier poets. It is in this character that
Chaucer's first dreamer pursues the whelp as it flees through a
forest whose rich grass, flowers and great trees are directly borrowed from the garden of de Lorris' seminal poem, and again
when he encounters the mourning knight in the depths of the
wood. As he apologises for intruding upon the stranger's privacy,
the dreamer seems to be acting as spokesman for an urbanely
civilised world whose graceful manners he has adopted instinc-
tively:

> 'A, goode sir, no fors,' quod y,
> 'I am ryght sory yif I have ought
> Destroubled yow out of your thought.
> Foryive it me, yif I have mystake.'   [BD 522–5

As we have already noticed, this speech reproduces a passage of
Machaut, from whom Chaucer is evidently learning the courtly

---

[1] Apparently his own, for the dreamer speaks of 'my bed' and 'my
chambre' and evidently knows where he is, though he describes the room
as if seeing it for the first time.

idiom as well as particular incidents of the typical love-vision.[1]
With Machaut's prompting, Chaucer is able to make his
dreamer speak with the authentic accent of *gentillesse*, but left to
his own resources he either finds this elegant form of speech too
elusive to capture or deliberately breaks away to the livelier
idiom of a less dignified level of society. It must be obvious that
when the dreamer rebukes the Man in Black for carrying grief
to such lengths, Chaucer is not attempting to reproduce the
characteristic manner of a courtier, but making the dreamer
speak in a manner which – on the face of things – is entirely
unfitting. Even if, as the dreamer absurdly supposes, the Man in
Black had lost nothing more valuable than a chess-piece, these
are not the terms in which a courtly speaker would conceivably
express himself to a faultlessly mannered stranger:

> 'Ryght thus
> Hath many another foly doon;
> And for Dalida died Sampson,
> That slough hymself with a piler.
> But ther is no man alyve her
> Wolde for a fers make this woo!'
>
> [BD 736–41

The courtly identity of the dreamer has been dropped, to be
replaced by a character which combines the earlier colloquial
energy with the mental obtuseness that cannot grasp the sense of
the Man in Black's figurative expression, and which substitutes
for his previous ignorance a fairly detailed knowledge of legend
and mythology, though evidently a scornful one. The elements
of this uneven, and as yet unresolved, narrating figure – courtier, reader, ignoramus, and unromantic bourgeois critic –
which appear spasmodically in different episodes of *The Boke of
the Duchesse* are discernibly related to his counterpart in the two
succeeding dream-poems. There perhaps the reader dominates;
one showing an acquaintance with all the great poets and
chroniclers of antiquity, the other dedicating a day of uninter-
rupted study to the *Somnium Scipionis* with the rapt concentration

[1] See above, p. 55.

of a monk. The courtly aspect dwindles, and persists only in the gauche attempts to compose the 'bookys, songes, dytees, in ryme' looked for in a cultured and sensitive person. These attempts reveal another kind of ignorance than the illiteracy of the first dreamer, who evidently has not heard of Venus or Cupid; for the hopeful poet of the two later poems is temperamentally too withdrawn to know much about life at first hand, and relies on books to keep him informed. Yet although scholarly and wary of adventuring far from his library, he speaks for the most part in the idiom of common life; seldom associating himself with the courtly world through style and outlook. In this figure Chaucer evidently found a comic satisfaction, and perhaps a deeper imaginative fulfilment, which persisted even when he had exhausted the interests of the dream-poem; for the same bookish and unworldly narrator accompanies the pilgrims along the road to Canterbury.

An enquiry into the imaginative meaning of Chaucer's dream-poems, such as this book has attempted, seems bound to involve some consideration of the final work in which many of his lifelong interests take their ultimate form. The poetic unity of Chaucer's writing is nowhere more apparent than in the persistence of certain basic circumstances and central figures throughout the early poems, and at last as structural elements of *The Canterbury Tales*. The narrator of all these works – a storyteller of modest gifts, who is happiest when he is repeating other men's tales – is the most conspicuous of these common features. The idea of making him a hopeful but untalented poet seems not to have occurred to Chaucer until he came to write *The Hous of Fame*; for in *The Boke of the Duchesse* the only suggestion that the narrator may be a practising writer is made in the closing lines of the poem, when the dreamer decides to 'put this sweven in ryme' as soon as possible. By developing this hint in his next poem, Chaucer gives his second dreamer a more definite personality without the contradictions of his predecessor, and differing from him in respects which make Chaucer's comic purpose much more evident. The narrator of this long and complicated dream is a love-poet, laboriously plying his trade in the evenings after the 'rekenynges' of his daily work, but so limited in experience that he needs a vision of nothing more wonderful than common life, about whose affairs he is woefully ignorant. Instead of participating in the flood of existence which washes against his door, he dazes himself with book-learning far into the night, and except at mealtimes lives like a hermit. Such a shy pedant is an unlikely candidate for a dream of wonder, but because Jove decides to reward his well-meaning persistence the dreamer is seized by an overwhelming force and carried help-lessly into a crowded and totally unfamiliar world of experience. The disparity between his restricted personal life hitherto and the boundless scope of the dream, as between his timidity and the Eagle's lordly self-confidence, sharpens the comedy of the dreamer's suddenly transformed situation. Throughout most of what follows the dreamer remains absurdly out of his depth, and overshadowed by the great figures whose legendary fame makes him appear even more insignificant and incapable.

Not only the name 'Geffrey' but a strong impression of crea-tive pleasure in Book II of this poem suggest that here Chaucer reached a particular point of achievement, by realising not one but two characters with whom he finds a close personal associa-tion. Although the picture of the almost mute and half-terrified dreamer could only be related to Chaucer as a comic inversion of fact, this absurd counterpart of his creative self evidently gave the poet an imaginative satisfaction as well as the immediate amusement of self-parody. The same uncourtly version of the dreamer recurs in *The Parlement of Foules*, where his function is much the same. He too must rely upon his reading for the information about human affairs which his unadventurous mode of life does not provide. 'Al be that I knowe nat Love in dede,' he remarks defensively,

> Ne wot how that he quiteth folk here hyre,
> Yit happeth me ful ofte in bokes reede
> Of his myrakles and his crewel yre.   [PF 9–11

The well-disposed supernatural force which has watched his efforts to honour Love on this inadequate basis is not impressed by this dedication to mere reading, though Africanus speaks approvingly of the dreamer's absorbed interest in the dogeared pages from which he hopes to learn something new – not evidently about love. Like his counterpart in *The Hous of Fame*, he seems to be more of a bookworm than a poet, and partly for this reason his guide treats him with the same amused condescension. Africanus' blunt comment, 'although that thow be dul', implies that the dreamer's lack of wit is only too obvious; and his readiness to give the dreamer something to write about 'if thow haddest connyng for t'endite', qualifies the offer of help by doubting the dreamer's capabilities as poet. This shorter poem, barely one-third the length of *The Hous of Fame*, allows less room for comic preliminaries to the dream; but the narrator is clearly a development from the 'Geffrey' of the previous work in this genre: a little more dignified and mature, and rather less disconcertingly handled by his guide, but still the withdrawn, abstracted recluse whose reading is a substitute for the practical experience lost through shyness.

In *The Parlement* the dreamer's background is less certain than previously. From his opening remarks about the arduous and exacting service required of the lover we might suppose that he was speaking from inside the courtly circle; but apart from his later acknowledgement of his practical ignorance of the subject, his fascinated study of the *Somnium* suggests a different character, by temperament a scholar and no lover. His remarks on the way learning is kept alive by books both confirms this impression and modifies it, by expressing the sensible outlook and imperturbable manner of cheerful bourgeois life:

> For out of olde feldes, as men seyth,
> Cometh al this newe corn fro yer to yere,
> And out of olde bokes, in good feyth,
> Cometh al this newe science that men lere.
>
> [PF 22–5

His readiness to accept popular opinion, 'as men seyth', his use of a proverbial saying and the relaxed tone of the passage, all identify the speaker with an unpretentious social background where perhaps agriculture represents a more dependable reality than 'newe science', which he seems to regard with some mistrust. The impression is a mixed one, but whether we see the dreamer as a studious recluse or as a representative of the humdrum world of fact, the incongruity of admitting such a figure to the garden of the traditional love-vision makes his situation comic. His reluctance to enter the garden until Africanus thrusts him through the gates is explained by his guide's comment that since he has lost his taste for love, he has no place there. The experience that would be entirely proper to a genuine poet, who would also be the servant of Love, is granted to him with no attempt to disguise his comic unfitness for such a vision.

The subject of the dreamer's incompetence is raised again in a passage of *The Legend of Good Women* of special interest to the design of Chaucer's work. At the entrance of the god and his queen, the dreamer waits kneeling by the daisy to see what is to happen, and is eventually noticed by the god. 'At the laste,' he relates,

> This god of Love on me hys eyen caste,
> And seyde, 'Who kneleth there?'
>
> [LGW F. 311–12

The dreamer introduces himself and approaches, to be rebuked for his presumption in stationing himself so close to the flower. Not entirely crushed, the dreamer asks why he should be so slighted, and receives a direct answer:

> 'For thow,' quod he, 'art therto nothing able.'
>
> [LGW F. 320

He has proved himself the enemy of love, the god continues, by the writings and translations which have mocked its servants and discouraged others from devoting themselves to the cause. When Alceste rises to defend the dreamer, she concedes that he has written 'the Rose and ek Crisseyde', to which the god might understandably take exception; but she reminds him that the dreamer has also composed poems in the god's praise:

He made the book that hight the Hous of Fame,
And eek the Deeth of Blaunche the Duchesse,
And the Parlement of Foules, as I gesse,
And al the love of Palamon and Arcite.

[LGW F. 417–20

Although the dreamer's incompetence is now a matter of his temperamental aversion to the central subject of poetry rather than of his lack of talent, he is still under attack from a figure of authority comparable with the Eagle and Africanus, who describes him scornfully as 'nothing able'. This unequal relationship between poet and guide does not change substantially when Chaucer, having meanwhile abandoned the dream-poem and its conventions, joins the nine-and-twenty in their eventful pilgrimage across the Kentish countryside. His apology in *The General Prologue* for the inadequacies of his presentation – 'My wit is short, ye may wel understonde' – admits one of the shortcomings which he shares with two of the dreamers. When the Host's eye falls upon the poet for the first time, evidently astonished to find so inconsequential a figure among the company of aggressively individual pilgrims, the encounter in *The Legend of Good Women* begins to be re-enacted in comic terms:

And thanne at erst he looked upon me,
And seyde thus: 'What man artow?' quod he;
Thou lookest as thou woldest fynde an hare,
For evere upon the ground I se thee stare.
Approche neer, and looke up murily!'

[CT VII. 694–8

The parallel completes itself after the interruption of *Sir Thopas*, when like his counterpart in *The Legend* the poet asks why he should be treated so disrespectfully, and gets an equally straight answer:

'Why so?' quod I, 'Why wiltow lette me
Moore of my tale than another man,
Syn that it is the beste rym I kan?'
'By God,' quod he, 'for pleyly, at a word,
Thy drasty rymyng is nat worth a toord!'

[CT VII. 926–30

Like his counterpart in *The Legend*, the poet is able to retrieve something of his reputation through another tale, which curiously enough concerns another good woman, Dame Prudence. But his disconcerting brush with the Host leaves him indelibly marked as a comic figure, both in the talent which produces only 'rym dogerel' and in the personal oddity which the Host mockingly holds up for approval. Staring fixedly at the ground and making no conversation, the poet has been trying to conceal his desperate shyness under a show of mental abstraction; though the Host's remark about his seemingly 'elvyssh' face might imply the other-worldliness of a poet lost in his private imaginings. But if so, the poet can have very little hope of impressing his fellow-pilgrims by a show of remoteness after the Host's good-natured mockery of his physical appearance. 'Now war yow, sires, and lat this man have place!' the Host cries, focusing attention upon the one pilgrim who may have tried to pass unnoticed in the crowd,

> 'He in the waast is shape as wel as I;
> This were a popet in an arm t'enbrace
> For any woman, smal and fair of face.'
>
> [CT VII. 700–2

The joke about the poet's girth recalls the Eagle's complaint that his passenger is 'noyous for to carye', and helps to establish the imaginative kinship of Harry Bailly with this no less imposing figure of the earlier poem. Both he and the Eagle are endowed with dominating force and authority which only the rashest of subordinates would wish to dispute. 'Us thoughte it was noght worth to make it wys,' the poet explains, accounting for the pilgrims' almost hurried acceptance of the Host's proposal to accompany them; and although the dreamer in *The Hous of Fame* finds the courage to decline the Eagle's lesson in astrology, he too is in no position to offer his guide any other kind of resistance. Condemned by shyness and lack of any personal expertise to be the least outstanding member of the remarkable gathering, the pilgrim poet is at a still greater disadvantage; and his wretched *Sir Thopas* is crushed flat under the steamroller of the Host's ridicule and contempt. Like the Eagle and Africanus, who also disillusion their dreamers of any literary aspirations which they may have nourished, the Host gives energy and directness to his already unsparing comments by the colloquial vigour of his language; appropriately in his case, since he personifies the exuberant spirit of common life in which Chaucer found the natural basis of his comic outlook.

The most important link between the Host and these two earlier figures lies in their common function. All three act as guides. The Eagle and Africanus obviously derive from the spiritual instructor who takes charge of the dreamer during an *oraculum*, carrying or conducting him to a point which affords him a prospect of future events or a revelation of divine truth. The Host is a guide in a more literal sense, leading his group of pilgrims by Rochester and Sittingbourne towards the shrine of St Thomas, where perhaps the parallel with an *oraculum* acquires some relevance. If he offers the pilgrims no spiritual revelation or glimpse of the future, he shares this shortcoming with Africanus and the Eagle, whose common purpose is to provide a poet of limited experience with 'tydynges', or something worth writing about. The pilgrim poet who can boast of only one tale, 'a rym I lerned longe agoon', stands in need of the same assistance; and the stories which he hears along the road to Canterbury greatly extend his previously miserable repertoire. This is not to suggest that the story-telling competition is devised for his benefit, for until the Host casts about for a new beginning after the Prioress throws the company into a sober mood, he seems unaware of Chaucer's presence. None the less, like his predecessors, he provides the poet with the 'mater of to wryte' which, as he duly records it, becomes the matter of *The Canterbury Tales*. The effect of the Host's actions in organising and controlling the sequence of tales is to enrich the poet's experience, of men as of the varieties of literature, in a fashion which matches the dreamer's education in *The Hous of Fame* by 'tydynges'.

> Of werres, of pes, of mariages,
> Of reste, of labour, of viages,
> Of abood, of deeth, of lyf,   [HF 1961-3

reflecting every aspect of human existence. The relationship of the Host and his comic charge is both less particular and less explicit than the comparable associations of guide and dreamer, but the two have a quality in common which sets them apart from the nine-and-twenty whose tales the poet reports. The 'sondry folk' who assemble in the Tabard have formed themselves into a company before either he or the Host encounters them, and although they accept the poet as a fellow-pilgrim he remains outside and apart from the group, separated from them by his shyness and by the awe which he feels for such splendidly imposing beings. While they talk, dispute or threaten he watches, as much an observer of an alien world as the dreamer in *The Hous of Fame*, who exchanges barely a word with those whom he meets or studies. Like the jovial guide of the dream-poems, the Host does not belong to the original company; but he sets them in motion by suggesting a competition along the way, and despite several threats and challenges to his authority he maintains his mastery of the dynamic force which produces the tales reported by the poet. His relationship with the pilgrim reporter assumes a deeper interest when we remember that in point of fact the Host is acting as front for Chaucer by ordering and directing the sequence of tales. By acting as critic and censor, the Host carries out his unseen creator's purposes, and exhibits all the assurance and competence lacking in the poet whom he ridicules. If we are ready to suppose that the ancestral figure who guides the dreamer of an *oraculum* may represent some pre-cognitive power of the mind, called into action by a personal crisis, we may be willing to see the Host personifying the creative purpose which fashions the wild energies of imaginative impulse into the ordered happenings of the finished poem. Not every poet may need to exert so great a force to subdue the dynamic pressure which Chaucer represents in the rebelliously self-assertive story-tellers of his final work. The recurrence of such clashes between undisciplined excitement and a figure 'of gret auctorite' in his poems suggests that for him only a proportionate measure of critical control – benign, because always certain of its mastery – could check and give shape to the exuberant energies which repeatedly challenge or resist the Host's leadership. In the main design of *The Canterbury Tales* as in the two more developed dream-poems, part of Chaucer's subject is again his own experience of the creative process.

The basic similarities between dreamer and pilgrim poet, and between Harry Bailly and the earlier guides, suggest that in *The Canterbury Tales* Chaucer is continuing to follow an established design despite a fundamental change of subject-matter; and that his last great work should be regarded as a development of the dream-poems rather than as an entirely new venture. The 'elvyssh' poet is awake but hardly aware of his surroundings as he rides, lost in reverie and unspeaking until the Host winkles him out of his contemplation. He seems a pigmy, overshadowed by the larger than life-sized pilgrims who throng about him, dazzling him by their professional eminence or personal vitality, or by achievements which he cannot hope to emulate. The disparity between this human nonentity and the fabulous beings who descend upon the Tabard is a condition of Chaucer's work which we have encountered before. It duplicates the experience of all his dreamers, who are unexpectedly confronted by indescribably noble or beautiful figures taken from classical history or romantic legend. In *The Boke of the Duchesse* they form the decoration in the sleeper's bedchamber which delights him upon waking; and in *The Hous of Fame* they fill a temple with such 'noblesse of images' that the dreamer is left dazed by their craftsmanship. A similar pleasure awaits him in the hall of Fame's house, filled with statues of famous poets and writers of history. The third of Chaucer's dreamers sees a more conventional display of figures associated with love, closer in type to the personified qualities which are described in the opening episode of the *Roman de la Rose*. But in *The Parlement* a second vision unfolds itself in the noise and disorder of quarrelling birds: a scene which contrasts strongly with the charming mythological *tableaux* in the garden, where beauty is untouched by time. Like the similar episode at the end of *The Hous of Fame*, the vision of a noisily animated crowd of plebeian figures, each eager to express his opinion or to tell his story, sweeps away the dreamer's impression of the dignified and motionless figures which he sees in the opening phase of his dream; and the silent ideal is replaced by the raucous voice of comic actuality. This development characterises the steady change of imaginative outlook over the course of Chaucer's poetic career. Even *The Boke of the Duchesse*, whose courtly world is only occasionally shaken by tremors of more vigorous activity, betrays Chaucer's interest in poetry of a less conventional kind, which would allow him to represent the texture of natural life and impulse, whose inclinations are towards comedy. The similar situations in the two subsequent dream-poems, where the dreamer is deafened by the noise of an unruly lower-class mob, underline this interest and point almost explicitly ahead to the poem in which another assembly of talkers and story-tellers will squabble over precedence, to be rebuked and kept in order by the master-figure to whom Chaucer lends his own authorial powers. There is no sudden or final break with the past. Rather, an element of his poetry becomes imaginatively dominant and absorbs Chaucer's interest almost completely. But the figure of the dreamer persists in the poet's new world, thrust incongruously into the waking reality which as bookworm he prefers to avoid, the astonished observer of creatures and events beyond his modest comprehension, who can only record what he hears and sees during his marvellous adventure.